My Two Fathers

Reviews of *My Two Fathers*

If you want to read a pastoral perspective—testimony would be the correct word if it weren't so old-fashioned and out of vogue—of a minister sure of his voice and witness, read anything by Terry Austin. You will get the unvarnished version, before the marketing lathe has been applied to the brutal confessional plaster. Terry is the quintessential Baptist preacher—one of our very best—unadorned by contrivances of ego or popular appeal, armed not with shiny ecclesial trappings but only with the Word of God. This book is about a son and a father, inextricably bound in love one for another, but with a rawboned frontier Baptist sensibility that shirks any sentimentality. A remarkable memoir, told in a voice so true and pitch perfect that you will long for a church, and a pastor, with such purity of heart. An essential reading for anyone trying to make sense of father and family, and what that has to do with God.

Charles Foster Johnson
Pastor, Bread Fellowship of Fort Worth
Executive Director, Pastors for Texas Children

"The book was a really hard read for me because the second 25 years of my life with my dad didn't go well. The book helped me dig into that and step back into working through my lost relationship with my dad. "My Two Fathers" is moving, inspiring, and challenging. As a dad, I'm reminded that I need

to show up like that for my kids. I was drawn to Terry's dad and sorry that I never had the opportunity to know him. God revealed himself to Terry in a lot of ways through his father and the book helped me see a number of ways that God revealed himself to me in spite of my dad and his issues, and that was a great realization. I was touched and moved in so many ways by how Terry's dad showed up and how he modeled Jesus."

**Geoffrey Bray
Elder, Mosaic Church, Fort Worth, TX**

My Two Fathers

Things My Earthly Father Taught Me About My Heavenly Father

Terry Austin

Copyright © 2020 by Terry Austin

All rights reserved. No part of this publication may be reproduced or transmitted in any form or by any means electronic or mechanical, including photocopy, recording, or any information storage and retrieval system now known or to be invented, without permission in writing from the publisher, except by a reviewer who wishes to quote brief passages in connection with a review written for inclusion in a magazine, newspaper, broadcast, or online publication.

Austin, Terry
My Two Fathers: Things My Earthly Father Taught Me About My Heavenly Father

ISBN: 978-1-7333130-4-9
Library of Congress Control Number: 2020934627
Categories: Fatherhood
Christian Inspirational

All scripture quotations taken from the New American Standard Bible (NASB),
Copyright © 1960, 1962, 1963, 1968, 1971, 1972, 1973, 1975, 1977, 1995 by The Lockman Foundation
Used by permission. www.Lockman.org"

Published in the United States by
Austin Brothers Publishing
Fort Worth, TX 76137

Books are available in quantity for promotional or premium use. Contact Austin Brothers Publishing
www.abpbooks.com

Bill Austin
October 30, 1925 – November 12, 2011

Introduction	1
Can't Say Can't	11
The Meaning of Sacrifice	25
How to Reverence God	43
Importance of Sticking to Your Principles	53
Keep Loving People	63
Always Trust God	77
Overcoming Obstacles	93
The Church is Worthy of Sacrifice	107
Conclusion	119
Appendix: Bill Austin's Eulogy	125

Foreword

In 1959, I had just graduated from the seminary and moved to Colorado Springs, Colorado, to begin pastoring my first full-time church with hardly a clue to what all that meant. The first week there, I attended the weekly pastors' fellowship of all the Baptist pastors in the area. I must admit I was a little intimidated by these experienced men who had been there for a time. A big man with an even bigger smile walked over to me, thrust out his hand, and said, "I am Bill Austin, and I want to welcome you to our fellowship." I recognized the name because our paths had briefly crossed at Howard Payne University before he had to drop out. A mutual friend, B.L. Davis, had shared his story with me also as we traveled to seminary together.

Bill and B.L. were part of a group of men from West Texas who had come back from the war with scars, seen and unseen, married but open to the call of Jesus to preach His gospel. Bill, like the others, responded with passion and dedication and became a force for the Lord, which eventually led him to churches in Colorado.

During the time I was there, he became a source of advice and help, which helped me through some rough spots. I will always be grateful.

This book, written by his son, Terry, describes well the influence that he had on his son and the lessons learned about the Heavenly Father from his earthly father. I have also had the privilege of knowing Terry from the time as a boy in Colorado to serving as a fellow pastor in the panhandle of Texas and later being fellow workers for the Baptist General Convention of Texas. I have seen his tenacity in fighting to keep his crippling handicap from polio as a child from slowing him down in his quest to live a full and productive life. His humor, spirit of caring, and deep commitment to the Lord have made that a reality.

You will also see in this book his obvious writing skills, which many of us in the small Trans-Canadian Baptist Association discovered years ago. Terry was elected as Clerk for the association with the responsibility of keeping the minutes. This was the most boring of the meetings, and he decided to liven it up. The monthly rendition of the minutes became something we looked forward to with eagerness. With humor and sometimes biting sarcasm, using many styles, he made us laugh at ourselves. And we loved it!

I think this book illustrates so well the influence which fathers have on their sons as well as the responsibility of demonstrating good principles of life and faith before them. Bill did this, and with Terry, it took.

Ed Rogers
Retired, Georgetown, Texas

Introduction

And we know that all things work together for good to them that love God, to them who are the called according to his purpose. For whom he did foreknow, he also did predestinate to be conformed to the image of his Son, that he might be the firstborn among many brethren. Moreover whom he did predestinate, them he also called: and whom he called, them he also justified: and whom he justified, them he also glorified. What shall we then say to these things? If God be for us, who can be against us? He that spared not his own Son, but delivered him up for us all, how shall he not with him also freely give us all things? Romans 8:28-32 (KJV)

I'm not sure I can separate my earliest memories of my father from my earliest memories of God. For most of my life, they were the same.

That might sound shocking to some, and I expect to be questioned by a few people for making that statement, so I probably need to explain. When most Christians envision God, they conjure up an image of Jesus only bigger and more (more of what I'm not sure). We've all heard that Jesus was God embodied within a man; He was God in the flesh. It stands to reason that God must look something like Jesus, only older since Jesus referred to God as His father. That's probably why many people's image of God is an old man, kind of like George Burns in the movie, *Oh, God*.

If you want to be more politically correct, you will come up with Morgan Freeman from *Bruce Almighty* or Whoopie Goldberg in *A Little Bit of Heaven*. When I was a young kid, we didn't go to the movies or watch TV, so I didn't have any help with understanding God and what He might be like other than what I was told and saw with my own eyes. Kind of like a baby kitten adopted by a mama dog, I grew up thinking God was like the one who cared for me and provided my needs.

That might be a good enough explanation for the first four or five years of my life, but there had to have been a time when I finally wised up and realized my father was nothing like God. Once I read enough of the Bible and understood the true qualities of God, I would cast aside such childish thinking—but I never did.

As I near completion of the seventh decade of my life, my declaration is the same—the person who taught me the most about God is my father. Every experience I've had with God has been seen through a lens of what my father taught or showed by his life. That doesn't mean my understanding of God is warped. I hope to show you throughout this book that my earthly father provided a thorough and healthy view of my heavenly father.

It has been understood for a long time that all of us are influenced by our earthly father when it comes to our concept of God. Church reformer Martin Luther commented how it was difficult for him to pray the Model Pray that begins with "Our Father..." He testified that it was hard to see God as father because his earthly father was "stern and unrelenting." Many people have been drawn to God by their father, and many more have been driven away from God by their father.

There are as many different relationships between fathers and children as there are people. I understand that. I'm also fully aware that when it comes to my personal experience with my father, I am a person of great privilege. I won the lottery when it came to fathers.

Many grew up with an absentee father, or an abusive father, or a weak father, or one who was simply a jerk. If that is you, I encourage you not to put down this book. You will not be better served by a book written by someone who lived your same experience. In fact, this book is probably more important for you than others. Let me explain.

It was July 4, 2000, and our family was gathered at Glorieta Conference Center. At the time, I worked for the Baptist General Convention of Texas, and they planned an appropriate week of activities. Glorieta was a special place for our family. Many summers, we spent a week there. It doubled as a vacation and conference time. Our three boys were there often enough to know all the hiding and adventure places. Since the conference center was located in the Rocky Mountains of northern New Mexico, exhausting opportunities for adventure was impossible.

On this particular year, much of my extended family was there for the week—both my brothers and their families, along with my parents. Since it was Independence Day, a special evening picnic was planned. Not only was good food provided, but we also sang a few patriotic songs, prayers were offered for the nation, and all the veterans present were recognized. This is the part I especially remember.

During the evening, they singled out veterans who served in the different branches of the military. As they asked for former Marines to stand and be recognized, I steadied Daddy's folding lawn chair as he pushed himself to his feet.

As he aged, it was more and more difficult for Daddy to stand up straight, but on this particular occasion, he was as tall as I remembered when I was a kid. Daddy's size was something that always impressed me. I don't know if it was because I was so small and weak, but I considered him to be the strongest man around. As young children, I remember both Linda and me trying to arm wrestle him, but we could never even move his strong right arm.

It is not surprising that when it comes to remembering and honoring his life, strength is the first thing that comes to mind. Not only did Daddy stand strong, but he was the source of strength for so many other people.

Daddy was in the Marines and fought on the island of Iwo Jima. His service was a matter of pride for our family, even though he never spoke about the experience. We were never able to forget about it because Daddy suffered significant wounds and eventually lost his right leg as a result. He never allowed the missing limb to slow him down for most of his life, but this particular night at Glorieta came as he was getting older. At seventy-five-years, he was frequently looking for an easier way to do things.

It is hard to comprehend the amount of courage he possessed as he and his fellow Marines stormed the beaches of Iwo Jima. On that seemingly inconsequential dormant volcano in the middle of the Pacific Ocean, he suffered a loss that forever changed his life and impacted the lives of everyone who knew him. A mortar blast led to the eventual amputation of his right leg and one of the defining moments of his life.

More than three years in and out of the hospital, a tragic automobile accident in downtown Amarillo, a tornado ravaging their home just a few days after my sister's birth, the emotional struggle of dealing with the devastating effects of polio on his oldest son–none of these events deterred him, they only served to give him additional strength.

As Daddy and I sat together on that July evening, waiting for the sun to disappear behind the mountain, listening to the music, and watching people finish off the hamburgers and hot dogs, neither of us said much. However, at one point, he leaned over to me and said, "When I'm gone, I want you preach my funeral."

From the perspective of hindsight, it's clear what he was thinking. He was tired. Physically he was worn out from relying on the strength of only one leg for half a century. Emotionally he was exhausted from a life filled with numerous one-of-a-kind experiences that most of us never have. Sitting next to his oldest son, surrounded by much of his family, he was aware it was about time to say goodbye.

I wasn't there yet. In response to his question, I quickly replied, "We're not ready for that; you have a long time yet."

The next few moments were silent as neither of us spoke. I thought about what he said and what he really meant, and I thought about my thoughtless reply. Before we finished the evening, I told him I would be honored to preach his funeral, and there was no one who would do a better job.

From that moment, continuing for the next dozen years, I began to write Daddy's funeral sermon. I rehearsed thoughts when waking in the middle of the night or driving down the highway through desolate west Texas or sitting in a boring church service. It was obvious that one funeral sermon could not contain everything that needed to be said about my father. (You can read the eulogy in the Appendix.)

Daddy died on November 12, 2011, in the Veteran's Hospital in Amarillo, Texas. We all knew death was imminent, but I was not able to be there. I didn't want to be there. I didn't need to be there. I was not physically capable of making the trip from my home in Fort Worth to Amarillo. Several months earlier, after a year of whining and complaining by my mother, he moved her back to Amarillo, where they had lived before relocating to Fort Worth to be near the kids.

The day my brothers packed up my parents' stuff in the U-Haul, I told Daddy goodbye, and as Sharon and I drove home, I told her that was the last time I would see him. It was. We talked on the phone frequently the next few months. He was ready to go. Because I knew how tired he was, I was ready as well, even though my heart was broken. When my brother called to tell me he had died, I sobbed out loud. I remembered the only time I had ever heard my father sob—it was when he received a phone call that his father had died.

I think about Daddy often. Sometimes I catch myself reaching for the phone to call him, to ask a question, or just to hear a reassuring voice. Frequently, when I look down at my hands, I don't know why, but I see Daddy's hands. Mine are not strong like his, but something about the shape of my fingers and the texture of my skin reminds me of him.

Perhaps the hardest thing about Daddy being gone is the loss of security he provided. It sounds terrible to say, but I always knew that if God ever failed me, Daddy would be there. He wasn't in the habit of rescuing me, but he would if needed. He didn't bail me out of problems, but he would if I ever asked. He didn't lavish me with stuff; he didn't build me up with bloated praise, but I always knew he would be there for me. To be honest, that made it easier to trust God.

When he was gone, it was now just God and me.

My whole life, Daddy prepared me for that eventuality. He taught me how to live, how to listen to God, how to learn from life, how to lean on someone for strength, how to leap into the unknown, how to lay burdens down, and how to love. He gave me everything I needed to be the man God wants me to be. I've often said, my goal in life is to be half the man my father was. Time will tell, but if I don't reach that goal, it will be because I didn't learn the lessons he taught.

In our final conversation, just a few days before he died, I asked Daddy if he was concerned about the outcome of a recent biopsy. Without any reservation in his voice, Daddy said he was not worried. Then he added, "Romans 8:28 has always been true." *And we know that all things work together for good to them that love God, to them who are the called according to his purpose.*

That's why I began his funeral with that great passage from Romans. It's also the way I begin the journey described in this book. God took an amazing collection of experiences from my father's life and weaved them together to make something good. The following are the lessons he taught me.

Can't Say Can't

I can do all things through Christ who strengthens me. (Philippians 4:13)

Truth: God will never ask you to do anything you can't do.

When you're a kid, one of the best weapons in your arsenal is to say, "I can't." It's an objection that's always appropriate when asked to do something. It doesn't require any thought or explanation, just a visceral protest.

Seldom does it have anything to do with capability. In other words, for a kid to say, "I can't do something" is merely a way of expressing a preference. It means, "I don't want to do that" with the hope our inability will convince Mom or Dad as a valid reason for withdrawing their instructions.

In my case, pleading "I can't" should have been an acceptable excuse. I survived a bout with polio when I was approaching my first birthday. The residual effects included virtually no use of my legs and limited use of my arms. I got around the house by crawling, even after other kids my age had been walking for years. When it was time to start first grade, the March of Dimes provided a wheelchair that allowed me to go to school. Prior to that, my parents had to carry me if we went anywhere. Fortunately, I wasn't very big.

In spite of my severe physical limitations, my father never let me say, "I can't." If I ever trotted out the excuse, he quietly reminded me that we're not allowed to say, "I can't." I soon learned that I needed to come up with another excuse or do what I had been asked to do.

It might sound unreasonable that I was not allowed to claim inability when asked to do something. However, it makes sense when you realize my father never asked me to do anything that I couldn't do. His requests were always doable. That doesn't mean I wanted to do them or that I always obeyed; it just meant I had to find another excuse.

Daddy's refusal to let me avoid doing things didn't stop after I got old enough to quit saying, "I can't." He continually encouraged me to try things, especially challenging things that pushed the boundaries of my limitations. There was no hesitation when it was time for me to attend school. My weakened condition was never a factor. My parents never asked for or expected special treatment for me.

I remember wanting to join the Cub Scouts while I attended Ben Franklin elementary school in Colorado Springs. We filled out all the forms and turned them in. The Scout Master called and asked if he could speak with my parents. I listened as he told my father that he would not be able to allow me to join the Scouts because I was in a wheelchair. He said they were not prepared to do what was necessary, and I would be unable to participate in many of their activities.

Daddy didn't say much as he listened. But he got angry. In fact, it's one of the few times I ever saw him angry. As a kid, I kind of expected him to throw a few punches and toss the man out of the house. Obviously, he didn't do that, but there was no doubt in anyone's mind that he was upset. As I think back on that episode, I realize he was angry because they were telling me that I can't do something, which was in direct opposition to what he had always taught me.

Rather than stewing about the situation and lashing out at the system, Daddy found a better way for me to get the benefits of scouting. He led the church where he was pastor to utilize a Baptist program for boys that included crafts, leadership, camping, and the added benefit of scripture memory. I remained a part of that organization for many years and attained some of the highest levels.

This was all a part of the process of learning that even if something is not available, there are likely other avenues to achieve the same result. I developed the mindset not to be afraid to try anything. In fact, Daddy frequently told me that whenever I fell down, he would be there to pick me up. He was. You can understand how easy it was to transfer that same concept to God.

By refusing to allow me to say, "I can't," he provided a powerful lesson that has paid enormous benefits in my relationship with God. Not only did I learn not to say the phrase, but I also learned to embrace the reality. Whenever God leads me to do something, I believe He will make it possible.

When I was about twenty-two years old, I was working a decent job and trying to determine the direction of my life. I had made a commitment early in the year to read through the entire Bible and was making good progress. Thoughts that God wanted me to be a pastor were becoming more and more frequent, but I shoved them aside.

Since Daddy was a pastor, I knew many of the inner workings of the job, and it didn't interest me. I also knew how hard he worked at making home visits, and that made it impossible for me. In Colorado, most houses had three or four steps into the front door, and I didn't do stairs.

Sitting at my desk one Sunday afternoon, I was trying to catch up on my Bible reading plan. The idea of being a pastor was nagging at me despite my well-reasoned objections. I came across a verse that struck me between the eyes like a sledgehammer. Philippians 4:13 says, "I can do all things through Christ who strengthens me."

Many who have felt God's call to ministry testify of similar experiences of God speaking in a clear, unmistakable manner. In my case, God was reaffirming what my father had always taught, I can't say, "I can't." My struggle was not about what God wanted me to do; it was about my belief I could do it. Up to this point, I had not spoken with my father about God's call because I knew my excuse would not carry any weight with him.

Something surprising happened when, finally, I did tell my father. Without hesitation, he replied that he had known for a long time. He never explained why he had kept quiet, but I knew. He wanted my call to come from God, not from him. In remaining quiet, he expressed confidence in God and in me. He had no doubt I could do what God was asking me to do.

Knowing that I could not say, "I can't" to God was a valuable commodity over the coming years. The first step was to complete my college education, so I enrolled at Wayland College in Plainview, Texas, the nearest Baptist college. Upon arrival, I discovered they did not have any dorm rooms that were wheelchair accessible. After the first month, I was moved to another dorm that was capable of being adapted and made accessible.

On the first day of classes, I met the young man who was to become my best friend throughout college. We realized we had identical schedules, and he offered to help me get around from class to class. Other students and friends were always quick to lend a hand whenever I encountered an obstacle.

One of my classes took a field trip to a Seminary where many of us would be headed upon graduation. I sat next to the head of the Religion Department as we rode the bus, and specifically asked if it would be possible for me to pastor a church. He told me it would be hard and wasn't sure it would happen.

When it came time to go to Seminary, Sharon and I chose one that was a thousand miles away, and its most distinguishing feature was its age—approaching one hundred years. The place was even less accessible than the college campus. Once again, students were always available to make it happen. When we arrived to move into our campus apartment, our new neighbor had been advised I might need help, and he did everything for us for the next few years and they became our best friends.

I can identify an individual at every place I have lived who became the person for me that I needed. In college, it was Keith, at seminary it was Fred, at my first church it was Alan. These men all became my arms and legs that helped make "all things possible."

When we moved to Fort Worth, I began to look around for the person God had prepared to pick up the slack for me, but he never showed up. Then it dawned on me; that person was my oldest son, Jeremy. He was 14 years old, strong, and more than willing. It's not an accident that God gave us three strong sons, and each has been there for me physically when needed.

The ministry job I took in Fort Worth involved preaching in different churches every Sunday in various cities throughout Texas. In case you are not aware, Texas is an enormous place, and churches can be found behind every tree in east Texas and next to every scrub bush in west Texas. Most Sundays were filled with preaching in one church on Sunday morning and then traveling to another church for the evening service. It was a grueling schedule for an able-bodied person, but for me, it was especially taxing.

Recognizing the situation, my son Jeremy took the initiative and asked if he could travel with me. I wasn't sure how serious he was or if it would last, but he proved more than capable of being God's provision. Nearly every weekend, we climbed into the car and headed off to a new church. Sometimes it was far enough away that we left on Saturday night and returned home late on Sunday. On more than one occasion, I was so exhausted that he would actually carry me into the house.

Every church had stairs to get on the podium and stand behind the pulpit. Jeremy and I became a coordinated team as he would deftly carry me up the stairs and stand me up in a position to speak. In addition, he became the subject of conversation as people noticed that my son was my helper. For years, I often encountered people who had heard me preach, and they would ask about Jeremy.

People noticed, and when I opened my mouth to speak, I already had their attention. God's faithfulness in providing my need gave credibility when I spoke about a God who could be trusted. The Apostle Paul spoke about a "thorn in the flesh" as a weakness of some kind that caused him to struggle with doing God's will.

Because of the surpassing greatness of the revelations, for this reason, to keep me from exalting myself, there was given me a thorn in the flesh, a messenger of Satan to torment me—to keep me from exalting myself! Concerning this I implored the Lord three times that it might leave me. And He has said to me, "My grace is sufficient for you, for power is perfected in weakness." Most gladly, therefore, I will rather boast about my weaknesses, so that the power of Christ may dwell in me. Therefore I am well content with weaknesses, with insults, with distresses, with persecutions, with difficulties, for Christ's sake; for when I am weak, then I am strong. (2 Corinthians 12:7-10)

There has been a lot of speculation over the centuries about Paul's thorn in his flesh. Although we can't be sure what it was, we do know it made life hard, and he wanted it to be gone. In fact, he specifically prayed three times for God to remove it. At some point, he quit praying and accepted the fact that life is hard.

Apparently, this is not a very popular opinion given the plethora of books and sermons that promise to teach us how God will solve any difficulty and make us successful. Name any subject you choose, and you can find a resource to teach you how to do it successfully. It seems that many have figured out life, and it can be taught to others. Honestly, I do not know how to be successful at much of anything because I have discovered that life is hard.

For the first fifty-five years of my life, every morning when I got dressed, the first thing I did was strap on a set of leg braces. If you remember the movie *Forrest Gump* and the braces he wore as a child, that is what I wore most of my life. Almost every morning, I had the thought, "I wish I did not have to put these things on!" Even though I no longer wear the braces, it still bothers me that it takes thirty minutes to get dressed in the morning when most people can do it in five minutes.

Every move I make physically requires greater effort than most people. The simple act of reaching up and flipping a light switch often requires me to use both arms after getting situated in the right position. My life has been full of leg braces, crutches, wheelchairs, obstacles, impossible barriers, doctor visits, and other fun things. Life is hard and getting harder every year.

I do not explain my problems to gain sympathy but simply to clarify the challenges that life has thrown my way. Yet, I am not alone in facing hardships. One thing I have learned is that every person faces their own unique set of challenges. Many of mine are very visible and the majority of yours might be unseen. However, just because of the simple fact that we live in a physical world with physical bodies and that we care about other people means that we live with difficulties. Life is hard!

When you love someone, it means that you also take on their hardships. If you are not aware of that, then you have not had children. Your children's struggles become your struggles, beginning with their very first breath through kindergarten disagreements to unemployment as an adult and every other difficulty they face. Life would be easier if we did not care about anyone but ourselves, but then it would not be worth living.

Every physical struggle I have had pales in comparison to the difficulty of seeing our one-month-old son (Andrew) lying in a hospital bed with meningitis, or our two-year-old (Matthew) get bit on the thumb by a rattlesnake, or having Sharon diagnosed with cancer, or having to leave a church unexpectedly after years of faithful service, or walking with Jeremy through a divorce, or numerous financial challenges, or a myriad of other experiences. One of the few things I know for certain is that life is hard!

If you believe that following God means He will smooth it out and make life easy, you're in for a rude awakening. Life is hard for everyone but especially for those who choose to follow Jesus. However, there is no need to give up and say, "I can't." Like Paul, we can.

He discovered not only that life is hard, but also that God is good. Once it was clear that God wasn't going to remove the thorn in Paul's life, Paul realized an even greater resource—the grace of God. God answered Paul's prayer by saying, "I'm not going to remove your thorn in the flesh.

Instead, I want to remind you that My grace is sufficient, for power is perfected in weakness."

That's what I learned from needing my son to put me on stage before I could preach. That's what I learned when moving to a new place and finding immovable obstacles. That's what I learned every time someone tried to discourage me by offering the excuse of my physical handicap. That's what I learned when my father taught me never to say, "I can't."

When you refuse to say, "I can't," you are in a position for God to turn your weakness into a strength.

While serving as pastor of a rural church in Texas, I invited a man from a mission organization to speak to our congregation on a Sunday evening. He was putting together a team to spend ten days in Brazil, preaching and sharing the Gospel. We had a good group attend that night, and the man did a marvelous job challenging us to be involved.

As everyone was filing out the door at the conclusion, I stood in the back of the auditorium and waited to greet our visiting speaker. After I thanked him for coming, I tried to encourage him by expressing confidence that some of our people would join his team for the trip. Almost without taking a breath, he turned it around on me by saying, "What about you? Are you going?"

I hadn't given it any thought. How could I make a trip to Rio De Janeiro when I could barely maneuver the flat plains of west Texas. I know I must have stuttered as I replied, "I can't go."

His response was sharp and straight to the point, "Have you prayed about it?"

I confessed that I had not, and later I had to ask God to forgive me for saying, "I can't."

Sharon and I went home and began praying that night. It didn't take long before we felt this is what God wanted for us. Not only did he encourage us about the physical obstacles, but within a few weeks, He also provided the financial resources necessary.

Looking back many years later, it's clear that the trip to Brazil was one of the highlights of our lives. God did some amazing things and provided in remarkable ways. As we rode the bus from our hotel on the beach to the inner-city church where we would labor for the next ten days, I was stunned by the steep hills where people lived. Sensing my concern, the team leader, the man who had challenged me to pray, sat down next to me and said, "Terry, what do you think?"

"It's going to be interesting," was all I could say. And it was.

At the church, a muscular young man took off from work to help me get around the entire time. He carried me everywhere we went. If necessary, he picked me up from the car, toted me into the house, and sat me down on the couch. We went up and down steep hills and over obstacles to visit people in their homes. I walked far less during our time in Brazil than I typically did at home.

The church we worked with was probably the only church in the city with a van large enough to carry my wheelchair. After being treated like royalty, it was hard to think about returning home, and if it wasn't for the fact our boys were still in Texas, we might have stayed.

At the closing rally, our team leader spoke with the pastor we worked with to see how it went. The pastor told him I was "Superman." That's an incredible thing to say about a man who had to be lifted and carried every place we went. It's precisely what Paul said— "when I am weak, then I am strong."

God has never asked me to do something I could not do. He has asked me to do some hard things, but I've learned that I can do all things through Christ who strengthens me.

The Meaning of Sacrifice

Some time later God tested Abraham. He said to him, "Abraham!"

"Here I am," he replied.

Then God said, "Take your son, your only son, whom you love—Isaac—and go to the region of Moriah. Sacrifice him there as a burnt offering on a mountain I will show you."

Early the next morning Abraham got up and loaded his donkey. He took with him two of his servants and his son Isaac. When he had cut enough wood for the burnt offering, he set out for the place God had told him about. On the third day Abraham looked up and saw the place in the distance. He said to his servants, "Stay here with the donkey while I and the boy go over there. We will worship and then we will come back to you."

Abraham took the wood for the burnt offering and placed it on his son Isaac, and he himself carried the fire and the knife. As the two of them went on together, Isaac spoke up and said to his father Abraham, "Father?"

"Yes, my son?" Abraham replied.

"The fire and wood are here," Isaac said, "but where is the lamb for the burnt offering?" Abraham answered, "God himself will provide the lamb for the burnt offering, my son." And the two of them went on together.

When they reached the place God had told him about, Abraham built an altar there and arranged the wood on it. He bound his son Isaac and laid him on the altar, on top of the wood.

Then he reached out his hand and took the knife to slay his son. (Genesis 22:1-10)

Truth: God made the ultimate sacrifice for us.

Over a period of more than 30 years, I preached hundreds, probably thousands of sermons. I have written sermons on every subject imaginable, and from every book in the Bible. I don't need to wade through all those sermon notes to be able to tell you there is one familiar passage of scripture that gets nothing but silence from me. It's the passage quoted at the beginning of the chapter—Genesis 22 and the story of Abraham offering his son as a sacrifice.

My avoidance has not been from a lack of interest or disagreement with the teaching. I know the story very well and have read books and commentaries in order to wrap my mind around what took place on that mountain in Moriah.

The reason for my hesitancy stems from the awesomeness of what Abraham was doing. As a father, I can't understand how a father could make this gesture, even after hearing a clear word from God Himself. I'm not sure we can fully comprehend what it means to sacrifice something.

One thing I do know is that sacrifice is a powerful thing. People making a sacrifice can change the course of a person's life. God's sacrifice of His only Son changed the world. The reason I don't preach from this passage is fear that I might say something flippant. Sacrifice has played such an important role in my life that I don't want to lead anyone astray. In fact, I think it's because the concept of sacrifice cannot be explained; it can only be experienced.

Late in May of 1968, on a Sunday afternoon, I graduated from High School. It was a memorable experience for several reasons. First, graduation is one of the most significant milestones in anyone's life. It comes at a time in life when we stare at the potential of the future in the face and say, "Here I come!" Doing it with others who have been friends for four or more years adds to the specialness of the day. Everything is good on graduation day.

The second reason is that early in the evening, a few hours after walking across the stage and getting my diploma, I checked in as a patient at Children's Hospital in Denver. It was a planned event. The plan was to have three surgeries designed to lessen the impact of polio on my body. Early Monday morning, they operated on my left foot. It involved cutting three notches in my bone to allow my foot to be straightened. My foot was placed in a plaster cast until the bone healed with my foot in the new position. On Wednesday morning, the process was repeated on my right foot.

Two days later, I was hung from the ceiling by a sling holding my head. The purpose was to allow gravity to pull my spine straight. Once it was as straight as possible, my entire body was wrapped in a plaster cast to hold the spine. A hinge was added on the right side of the cast. Every morning, the doctor would come to my room and twist the hinge a few times, forcing my back to move even further in hopes of getting it as straight as possible.

I was lying in a hospital bed wrapped in plaster with only my head sticking out on top, my arms were free, and my toes were showing. Daily, the doctor would increase the torque on my spine. The plan was for him to keep going until I said enough. This went on for about two weeks, and it was obvious I was closing in on my limit.

My mother came to the hospital every day, and Daddy came by every couple of days whenever he could get away from work. One afternoon he was sitting at the side of my bed when Dr. Matchett came by to check on his patient. Dr. Matchett had been my doctor for many years and he and daddy got along well. I think it was their shared experiences from the war. Daddy fought in the pacific and Dr. Matchett was a military physician in Europe. His bedside manner gave evidence of practice on the battlefield.

The surgical plan was to chisel bone chips from my thigh and lay them on my spine to cause my spine to be fused into one straight piece. We all knew it was about time for that final phase. Dr. Matchett, addressing my father more than me, said he was worried about doing the surgery. He was afraid my skinny legs didn't have enough bone to provide what was needed for my spine. That was extremely discouraging. It meant the entire summer of misery had been a waste. It sounded like they might have to cut the casts off and send me home in the same condition I was in at the beginning.

My Dad heard the doctor's words and immediately spoke up. "Can you take the bone from me?" he asked.

Dr. Matchett hesitated for a moment and replied, "I don't know why not."

He went on to explain that he had never done it before but didn't see any reason why it wouldn't work.

In order to understand why I'm telling this story in a chapter about sacrifice, you need to remember that my father only had one leg. His right leg was amputated 25 years earlier, and now he was offering to allow the doctor to chisel bone fragments from his left hip because I needed the bone. My best attempts to talk him out of doing it were barely heard. They immediately begin planning the procedure. Daddy would check into a different hospital (remember, I was in Children's Hospital), and Dr. Matchett would take his bone early in the morning, bring it over to my hospital and stick it in my spine early in the afternoon.

The operation was harder on Daddy than me. I barely felt any pain, just a little discomfort from a long incision. He felt the pain of having bone scraped from his hip. In fact, it took him several months to return to normal.

I survived the summer. The casts were removed, and I was able to start college for the fall semester with a stronger spine and straighter feet. However, neither Daddy nor I ever forgot the experience. For the rest of his life, he would occasionally tell people that I was "bone of his bone." He loved to say that even though he and I were often the only ones who knew what it meant.

When it comes to teaching me about God, reflect on what my father showed me during the summer of 1968. He provided a powerful demonstration of what it means to offer a sacrifice simply because you love someone. The concept of sacrifice is a frequent theme found throughout scripture, and an apparent quality possessed by God.

Sacrifice of our Rights

Abram was specially chosen by God to be the father of a nation. It's not surprising that his life was blessed in many ways. However, he was more than a privileged man who went about getting everything he could out of life. He was a man who understood a great deal about life. The ability to offer his son as a sacrifice did not occur in a vacuum. He already knew something about sacrifice.

Abram's family and fortunes were greatly blessed by God, both rapidly growing beyond what the land could sustain. He was in a position of power and privilege. It was his choice to make concerning who owned what and where they should live. His nephew Lot shared in that success, and his family and fortune also increased. The time came when it became obvious they could not thrive together.

So Abram said to Lot, "Let's not have any quarreling between you and me, or between your herders and mine, for we are close relatives. Is not the whole land before you? Let's part company. If you go to the left, I'll go to the right; if you go to the right, I'll go to the left."

Lot looked around and saw that the whole plain of the Jordan toward Zoar was well watered, like the garden of the Lord, like the land of Egypt. (This was before the Lord destroyed Sodom and Gomorrah.) So Lot chose for himself the whole plain of the Jordan and set out toward the east. The two men parted company: Abram lived in the land of Canaan, while Lot lived among the cities of the plain and pitched his tents near Sodom. (Genesis 13:8-12)

Abram suggested they part ways, and as the patriarch, he would be expected to choose the best property for himself. There was no reason for him to give up the best land. Yet, he did. Abram deferred to Lot to look around and chose the best location. He did. Abram settled for less, but God continued to bless him. Although he was not yet prepared to sacrifice his most precious possession, his son, he was already learning the power and blessing of sacrifice.

To sacrifice our rights and privileges is not a popular activity. I frequently hear Christians speak of their "God-given rights." As far as I know, God has not given us any rights. He has filled our lives with blessings, gifts, and privileges, but we don't have any rights. It is easy, and common, to confuse what God has given and what we are given as a citizen of a country.

I hear this often expressed when it comes to Second Amendment arguments. As a citizen of the U.S., we do enjoy certain rights when it comes to gun ownership. However, these rights as citizens do not transcend into our spiritual lives. The Christian life is not about claiming our rights. It's about sacrifice, of giving up what we have to God and to benefit others.

Even if there was such a thing as "God-given rights," the blessing does not come with gripping them firmly but with letting them go. Several years ago, I wrote a book titled *Authentic Stewardship*. The book was an expression of my concept of stewardship at the time. I intentionally put a photograph of a woman's open hands holding two small coins on the front cover. The reason is because the overarching theme of stewardship is that we are to live with open hands. Whatever God gives us, we are to open our hands and let it go if it is needed by someone else. We don't have the right to hold on to anything.

Sacrificial Giving

While He was in Bethany at the home of Simon the leper, and reclining at the table, there came a woman with an alabaster vial of very costly perfume of pure nard; and she broke the vial and poured it over His head. But some were indignantly remarking to one another, "Why has this perfume been wasted? For this perfume might have been sold for over three hundred denarii, and the money given to the poor." And they were scolding her. But Jesus said, "Let her alone; why do you bother her? She has done a good deed to Me. For you always have the poor with you, and whenever you wish you can do good to them; but you do not always have Me. She has done what she could; she has anointed My body beforehand for the burial. Truly I say to you, wherever the gospel is preached in the whole world, what this woman has done will also be spoken of in memory of her." (Mark 14:3-9)

On that day, Jesus said, "wherever the gospel is preached in the whole world, what this woman has done will also be spoken of in memory of her." Her giving was so amazing that people would talk about it forever. And here we are, talking about the gift.

This event took place in the home of a man named Simon, who is referred to as a leper. Likely, he did not currently suffer from leprosy because no one would have come to his home. Lepers were not allowed to live in towns or be in contact with other people. It is possible that he is known as Simon the leper because Jesus had healed him of his disease on a previous visit. He might have proudly accepted the designation of a leper because it was a perpetual testimony of Jesus' healing touch. Perhaps the hospitality was an expression of gratitude and celebration.

Jesus, his disciples, and some other friends were enjoying Simon's hospitality. They were reclining at a table, which is how they ate meals in those days. It sounds like it was a great time of fellowship, provided by a grateful host, and honored by the presence of the Son of God.

A woman entered the room with "an alabaster vial of very costly perfume of pure nard." Without going into all the detail of the terminology, let's just say that she had a very expensive bottle of perfume. In fact, its value is placed at 300 denarii, which is the equivalent of one year's wages for a common laborer. This bottle was worth about $30,000.

The woman broke the vial, which probably means that she broke the wax seal that kept the perfume from spilling. Then she did the unthinkable; she poured the perfume on Jesus' head, irretrievably spilling the precious liquid. It was an extravagant act of worship and adoration. Such a gift went beyond all wisdom and practicality.

When you look up the word "extravagant," you find terms like excessive, unrestrained, and recklessly wasteful. That is why extravagant giving always catches people's attention. I'm not talking about a multi-millionaire giving a few hundred thousand dollars to support a charity. Being extravagant has nothing to do with being rich.

In August of 2005, Sharon and I were attending a small congregation on a Sunday evening. The devastation of the Katrina hurricane was just becoming known, and people were trying to decipher the best way to respond. During that worship service, a young man, probably in his 20's, announced that he felt called to load up his pickup with supplies and head toward New Orleans to help people. He said that he was going to go as far as he could and help as many people along the way as possible.

During that same service, they took an offering so the rest of us could give something to the rescue efforts. We put in a check for $1,000 to be used at the church's discretion. At the conclusion of the evening, one of the elders asked if it would be acceptable to use the money we gave to help this young man go as God had called him. We were excited to be a part of his ministry.

I think this young man's gift of his time, vehicle, effort, and presence was a much more extravagant gift than my one-thousand dollars. It doesn't seem nearly as unexpected or daring for a middle-aged man to write a check as it does for a young man to set out on a journey, not knowing where it would lead.

You may not be wealthy, but you can still give a memorable gift. All it requires is that it be extravagant. All of us can do that.

One of the interesting features of the New Testament stories is that we can always identify with the characters. In this particular story, I like to think I am like the generous woman. However, if I am honest, I must confess that I am more like the sensible disciples. The disciples could not comprehend how such a valuable resource could simply be poured out on Jesus' head. Jesus was the great advocate for the poor and needy; there is no way that he would appreciate such an enormous waste of money. This would be like clearing out two acres of rain forest to build a house for Al Gore. The disciples were confident they would be praised for their stewardship insight. Three phrases describe the disciple's attitude.

They were "indignantly remarking to one another." The word "indignant" literally means that they had "much grief." They were really upset. They describe the woman's action as a "waste," which is a very strong term that means destruction or utter ruin. From their perspective, there was nothing positive about this woman's gift. They even gave the woman a public scolding. This term is filled with emotion.

Sometimes you get mad at something but not mad enough to say or do anything. But other times you get angry enough to act, to make a statement or take an action. This was one of those times for Jesus' disciples. This poor woman's extravagant gift had enraged Jesus' closest followers. The apparent reason for their anger is that this money could have been better spent by providing for the poor. They could not comprehend how anyone could take the equivalent of a year's income and use it in such a fashion, by wasting it on Jesus.

Now, if you don't think this is a common attitude today, the next time you talk to your neighbor, somehow work into the conversation that you are planning to give a percentage of your income to your church. Or, if you really want to get him riled up, talk about giving away an entire week's income to a ministry for needy families.

I can assure you that when you become a generous giver to God, there will be people in your life who misunderstand. People will not expect you to be giving to God when there are so many other things you could do with the money.

Let me describe a common experience when this occurs. Often, when a wealthy husband and wife choose to leave the bulk of their estate to a ministry, it is unexpected by the children. Some Christian financial planners schedule "family meetings" when this happens. The purpose of these meetings is for the husband and wife to tell the children about their plans. I can assure you that these meetings do not always go well. Many times, the children have a "better idea" about where the money should be spent.

Memorable giving will often be unexpected. The reason it is memorable is because it goes against the grain of expectations. If we follow the norm in our giving, there will be nothing memorable about it.

The disciples held the practical perspective and suggested that the money would have been better spent on the poor. However, Jesus did not see things the same way, which should not surprise us. He teaches the disciples about the spiritual implications of the woman's actions. He points them to the fact that she was anointing His body for burial. She was preparing Jesus for the sacrifice that He was to offer within the next few days. She demonstrated sacrifice.

This woman did something that she probably did not even understand herself. She was anointing Jesus' body for burial. She was giving all that she had as an act of worship. Her goal was to worship, and her response to the need for worship was to give. True worship will always elicit giving.

Tom White joined his father's construction business when he returned home from World War II. The company became very successful, growing from doing $10,000 excavations to $400 million construction jobs. However, what makes Tom memorable is that over a 25-year period, he gave away all of his stock in the company—stock that was worth about $200 million.

Tom explains, "When people ask me why, I say, I have two gifts from God: the gift of compassion, and the gift of making money. I just put them together, so they are hand in hand. My heart has always been with the underdog. Jesus is my role model. Some people think that God makes people rich because they are nice guys and that poor people must have done something wrong. I believe it is sinful to sit on millions...when you claim to know Jesus."

Sacrificial Living

About a quarter of a mile down the street behind my house, they're building a huge structure. It sits on the edge of a neighborhood of houses on one side and commercial property on the other. The three-story structure gets more and more imposing with each new day of construction. The purpose of this large structure is for storage, a place for people to keep the stuff that no longer fits in their house.

By the way, this is not the only storage facility nearby. On my street, few people can park two cars in their two-car garage. In fact, most can't even squeeze in one vehicle. The reason is that the garage has become an overflow for their stuff. But that's not enough. They build three-story storage places and rent them out so people can pay extra just to keep their stuff. All of us have too much.

About the only time we give serious consideration to downsizing is when we get old enough to discover that taking care of all the stuff requires too much energy. However, few people ever discover the value of sacrificial living. Let me define what I mean by that phrase. I'm referring to living below our means.

Sacrificial living means choosing a standard of living at a level below what we can afford. It might mean making repairs to an existing vehicle rather than buying a new one. Or, perhaps living in a smaller house than we can afford. There are countless ways to cut living expenses if you want to live below your means. Living sacrificially allows you to free up resources that can be used for God's kingdom. It might mean giving to a ministry, helping individuals, giving to neighbors in crisis; again, the possibilities are limitless.

> *Through Him then, let us continually offer up a sacrifice of praise to God, that is, the fruit of lips that give thanks to His name. And do not neglect doing good and sharing, for with such sacrifices God is pleased. (Hebrews 13:15-16)*

In Hebrews, we are encouraged to offer sacrifices of praise to God. However, it goes on to say that we should not neglect the sacrifices of "doing good and sharing." They are identified as sacrifices that please God. When we choose to live sacrificially, we put ourselves in a position to do good and share with others.

Ultimate Sacrifice

It's not possible to address the subject of sacrifice without a discussion about the ultimate sacrifice. At the beginning of Jesus' ministry in the world, John was preaching a message of repentance and turning to God. He pointed to one coming soon who will be the greatest of all men. As he was preaching one day, "he saw Jesus coming to him and said, 'Behold, the Lamb of God who takes away the sin of the world!'" (John 1:29).

The image of the Lamb of God is unmistakable. It is a reference to a sacrificial offering made in search of forgiveness. Jesus was the Lamb of God, which means He was God's sacrifice for the sins of all men. I don't pretend to understand what theologians call "atonement." In other words, I can't explain how Jesus' death on the cross made forgiveness of my sins possible, but the Bible is clear, that is what happened.

For God so loved the world, that He gave His only begotten Son, that whoever believes in Him shall not perish, but have eternal life. For God did not send the Son into the world to judge the world, but that the world might be saved through Him. (John 3:16-17)

God sacrificed His only Son for the benefit of humanity. It is the heart of the Gospel and the theme that runs throughout scripture, from Genesis to Revelation. If you don't understand sacrifice, then you know nothing about God. My father taught it to me. From as early as I can remember, he taught me about Jesus and His death on the cross. He also taught me by the way we lived. He gave up everything to follow God's call and taught the family how to live happily and meaningfully with very little of the world's possessions. On more than once occasion, I saw people in need come to the "preacher's house," and Daddy gave to help them out, not out of a church fund but out of his own pocket. He taught me about giving as he required us to put our own money in an envelope each Sunday morning as we went to church.

As I was covered in plaster from head to toe, it was not a surprise as I listened to my father offer bone fragments from his own hip because I needed them. He had been teaching me about sacrifice all my life—on that day, he showed me what it meant.

How to Reverence God

The fear of the LORD is the beginning of wisdom, And the knowledge of the Holy One is understanding. (Proverbs 9:10)

Truth: God is worthy of reverence from those who know Him.

Like many areas of my life, I was behind most kids in getting a driver's license. It didn't happen for me until I was 17. I don't recall it being a big deal that it took a year, but I know there must have been some disappointment. Looking back through the lens of my practical nature, I was probably aware maneuvering the pedals of a car was not possible, so I didn't expect to drive.

However, I do recall Daddy coming home one day to report that he had discovered that hand controls were available that allowed driving without the use of legs. It was like him to figure out a way to do something that didn't seem possible. If you're old enough, you might remember that cars had a switch on the floor to the left of the brake pedal. The purpose of that switch was to dim the headlights. The driver simply tapped the switch with his left foot and the lights would go from bright to dim when approaching another car.

Since Daddy only had one leg, he couldn't use that switch, so whenever he bought a car, he had to have a toggle switch installed on the dashboard to control the brightness of the lights. He also talked about a method he had in earlier times of using a stick to push in the clutch peddle. When you're handicapped, perhaps your best friend is resourcefulness.

Back to my story. As I approached my seventeenth birthday, Daddy had our family's second car equipped with hand controls so I could drive. Back in those days, Driver's Education was taught by the school, so I signed up. Getting through the classroom portion was not a problem, but when it came time to practice driving, some adjustments had to be made. My father arranged for Mr. Weigand, the Driver's Ed. Teacher, to bring me home from school on the days I was to drive. We got in our vehicle and he put me through the paces, just him and me. The man had a lot of courage, because unlike the regular Driver's Ed. car, he did not have a brake pedal he could use from the passenger's seat.

I passed the class, passed the driving test, and secured my license. All was now right with the world.

I remember the first time I was allowed to drive without my parents in the car. It was after church one Wednesday night. Daddy handed me the keys and told me that I could drive home by myself. The first thing I did was ask if I could drop my friend, Jim Grundy, at his house. Since it was on the route home, there was no objection. Jim and I got into the Ford Galaxy and headed out of the church parking lot.

Jim only lived a few blocks from the church, but by the time we reached his house, we had convinced ourselves that a girl from our church needed to see us that night. We drove past Jim's house and turned south on Washington street. While stopped at the traffic light at the intersection of 88th and Washington, a car pulled up beside us. Jim saw it first and then turned toward me with a frightened look on his face.

The car next to us was driven by my father. Dutifully, Jim rolled down the window and I looked over toward Daddy. He simply said, "We'll talk when you get home."

I'll admit, I was afraid. However, it was not the fear of a teenager caught deliberately disobeying his father. I was not afraid that he would hurt me, or even that he would punish me. Daddy never did anything to make my life painful or hard. Everything he did to and for me was always for my benefit. My fear was not of having to suffer in some way. I was afraid that I had disappointed him.

I loved and respected him and the idea of disappointing him was hard to accept. He had trusted me. I failed. I was afraid, not of him, but of what I had done to our relationship. That's what it means to fear God.

We are instructed countless times in the Bible that we are to fear God. Perhaps a better term would be "reverence" or "be in awe" of God. Some have developed a religion that suggests we should be afraid that God is going to send us to hell if we don't do certain things or live a certain way. In fact, this is a common approach to doing evangelism. We are encouraged to ask the question, "If you were to die tonight and God said, 'Why should I let you into heaven?' what would you say?"

That's not the kind of fear that my father taught me. In our house, God was not to be feared. He was to be reverenced. Because of my father's life and the way he treated me, I wanted to please him, not like a sycophant hoping to curry favors, but simply because I loved him. My father cared for me and provided everything I needed for life. Why would I not want to be pleasing to him.

I "feared" my father because of who he was to me. He gave me life (creator), and then he provided for that life (sustainer), and then he walked with me through that life (partner). This is precisely what God does for each of us. He is the creator, sustainer, and partner that makes our life possible. Once you become aware of this truth, the only option is to "fear" Him.

> *On that day, when evening came, He said to them, "Let us go over to the other side." Leaving the crowd, they took Him along with them in the boat, just as He was; and other boats were with Him. And there arose a fierce gale of wind, and the waves were breaking over the boat so much that the boat was already filling up. Jesus Himself was in the stern, asleep on the cushion; and they woke Him and said to Him, "Teacher, do You not care that we are perishing?" And He got up and rebuked the wind and said to the sea, "Hush, be still." And the wind died down and it became perfectly calm. And He said to them, "Why are you afraid? Do you still have no faith?" They became very much afraid and said to one another, "Who then is this, that even the wind and the sea obey Him?" (Mark 4:35-41)*

It's possible to learn this kind of fear without having an earthly father like mine. Jesus taught it to His disciples in memorable ways. Perhaps one of his best lessons was provided on the Sea of Galilee. After a long day of preaching and ministry, Jesus suggested they cross the water to the other side. Since several of his disciples were fishermen, this was something they could handle. The piled into a boat and several other boats sailed alongside.

While the little armada was in the deep part of the water, "a fierce gale of wind" came upon them. I don't know much about boating in the open water, but I do know it's probably not a good thing to be hit by a strong wind. Along with the wind came the waves. They were so high that they were breaking over the boat. This went on long enough that the boat was beginning to fill with water. That means the next step is to abandon ship before it sinks.

Before you agree with the disciple's assessment that they were about to drown, don't forget, Jesus was in the boat. Granted, he wasn't manning the oars to fight the wind, or bailing out water to prevent sinking, but he was with them. While they were in a panic for their safety, he was sleeping on a cushion in the back of the boat.

In my experience, it seems like God does this a lot. Sometimes it feels like He is kind of a drama queen, waiting to rush in the last minute to rescue us. I always want Him to solve a problem immediately. I'm impatient when it comes to fixing something. I don't like to analyze and study, I want to get it solved. I know the frustration they felt when the disciples said, "...do you not care that we are perishing?"

We've all said it— "God don't you care that I'm going under over here? What are you waiting for?"

What we fail to realize is that as long as Jesus is in the boat, it's not going to sink. The disciples felt it was necessary to wake Jesus and let Him know they were about to die. They didn't do it in such a way as to suggest He might do something. It's like they just wanted Him to know.

You can nearly feel His exasperation as He rose to His feet. When He was finally ready to say something, He didn't speak to the disciples. Instead, He spoke to the wind and the sea. That's right, He said, "Hush, be still." Immediately, the wind died down and the water became perfectly calm. With three short words, "hush, be still," He solved the problem.

At that point, he turned to the disciples to make sure they didn't overlook what had happened. He said, "Why are you afraid? Do you still have no faith?"

They had already witnessed Jesus heal several people, cast out demons, forgive a man's sins, and attract large crowds. Even though it was still the early days of His time in the flesh, they had seen enough to trust they were in good hands. Their faith was not mature at this point, but it had been quickened. Their faith should have been strong enough to overcome their fear.

I want to make an interesting point concerning Jesus' statement. He clearly associates fear and faith. It has often been said that fear is the opposite of faith. That is precisely what Jesus expressed in His two questions—"why are you afraid and where is your faith." When faith falters, the result will always be fear. When our faith is strong, our fear will be weak.

Jesus calmed the storm and asked the questions. The disciples, who were already afraid, suddenly became "very much afraid." Two different words are used. Jesus asked why they were "afraid," which comes from a term meaning "fear-driven." It suggests a dread of losing something; in this case, they were in fear of losing their life. It could easily be translated cowardly or timid.

However, after they saw Jesus calm the angry sea, it says they were "very much afraid." Two words are used that help us understand the meaning. The first is the word "mega." You know what that means. We use it all the time to describe something that is great. If something is "mega" it means it is massive, huge, impressive. The second term is "phobia." Again, this is a term familiar to most of us. We speak of a phobia as a fear. It is used as a suffix to describe various fears—hydrophobia is the fear of water.

This kind of fear doesn't make us cowardly or timid. Instead, it makes us act. If you suffer from hydrophobia, you will stay away from a boat or swimming pool. A person with acrophobia has a fear of heights and it will cause them to stay out of tall buildings or away from the edge of a mountain.

"Phobia" is the term used to describe our attitude toward God. We are frequently told to fear God. It is the idea of reverence or respect. This kind of fear causes us to do certain things and avoid other things. It is what I mean when I say I was afraid of my father. By my disobedient road trip, I had disrespected my father, and that is something I never wanted to do. He was worthy of my reverence and respect.

When the disciples witnessed Jesus speaking to the wind and waves, they were stunned. They were in awe, "very much afraid" because "even the wind and the sea obey him."

My father never calmed the water and the wind, but he provided everything I needed. He couldn't make my life easy, but he did make it possible. He couldn't relieve my disappointment over not being able to join the scouts, but he helped me find something much better. When I had accepted the possibility that I would not be able to operate a car, he went out and found a way to make it possible.

From him, I learned reverence and respect. I learned what it means to fear God.

When Daddy looked over at me and said, "We'll talk when we get home," I made a left turn and headed that direction. I remember sitting next to him at the stop light as clearly as what I had for lunch today, but I have no idea what he said when I got home. I'm sure he said something because he seldom let a teachable moment pass by. I'm sure I wasn't grounded because I don't remember ever being grounded.

It really doesn't matter what he said because I had already learned what I needed to learn. When you are loved, it's painful when you disappoint that person. I have spent a lifetime trying to relate to God in the same way I learned to relate to my father.

Importance of Sticking to Your Principles

"Also the Glory of Israel will not lie or change His mind; for He is not a man that He should change His mind." (1 Samuel 15:29)

Jesus Christ is the same yesterday and today and forever. (Hebrews 13:8)

Truth: God will always be consistent with who He is.

What's the next step when you finally give in to what you believe God wants you to do? By agreeing, you're backed into a corner in a sense. It's no longer possible to refuse, so you have to do the next best thing, get prepared. Sitting at the kitchen table for 20 years across from a preacher, I knew the requirements of being a preacher. Daddy didn't come home and complain about church members, but it was obvious that some of them worked their way under his skin. Working with people can be like working with produce. At first, it's fresh and colorful but after a while, they can get stale and even rotten. I wasn't ready to deal with that.

The first thing I did when I responded to God's call to preach was to figure out how to get the education I needed. The nearest Baptist college was in Plainview, Texas, about 300 miles away. No thought was given to anything other than a Baptist college because we were as much Baptist as we were Christian. We followed Jesus, the one who was baptized by John the Baptist. We were familiar with Wayland Baptist College because my sister had attended one semester there, so it was a simple decision.

In the meantime, it was a couple of months before the spring semester started, which gave me time to get my ducks in a row before starting my quest. The plan was to go to school to learn how to preach, something I desperately needed. Daddy decided to do his part to help me learn the art.

He arranged for me to preach my first sermon at a Sunday evening service of a small church. If you put those words together— "evening service" and "small church"— it's obvious that not many people were there to hear my first sermon. Nevertheless, I gave them all that I had. Like many preachers, I remember that first sermon. It had four points—you should love the Lord with all your heart, soul, mind, and strength. I'm aware I had no idea what that meant but that didn't affect my confidence. After a good ten minutes of laying out everything I knew about the Christian faith, I said a closing prayer, and we went home. It was a start.

College was great, and it was obvious that Wayland was accustomed to preparing young men for the ministry. Since a two-year degree was already on my resume, my schedule of classes was saturated with subjects that every pastor needs to master. Even the out-of-classroom activities were designed to prepare us to be leaders in the church.

Daddy was an encouragement, but not in a cheerleading sort of manner. Perhaps it was because he was not able to complete a college education, but I never got the sense he was fully behind the idea. Financially, he was not in a position to provide much help. I had two monthly car payments remaining, and he paid those for me, but he never provided any financial help while I was in school. I worked two jobs and carried a heavy class load and that might have been the lesson he wanted me to learn. I don't know. We never discussed it, and at no time did I expect him to pay my way. That's not the way he did things.

With a college degree in hand, it was obvious that being a successful pastor was still beyond my ability. I knew I wasn't ready. The next step was seminary, so off to Louisville, Kentucky, not 300 miles away like college, but closer to a thousand. I was getting older (mid-20s), and began to feel anxious, so I doubled down on the course load. Extra hours each semester, summers, and in between semester classes, allowed me to complete the three-year program in two-and-a-half. This time, as graduation neared, I was ready to take on a church.

I was ready, but God wasn't.

A couple of months before seminary graduation, Daddy asked if my plan was to return home to Colorado to preach. I had never considered any other option, and I expected he would be pleased. I assured him that I was excited about the possibility. Colorado was my home where I grew up and expected to live out my days in the mountain state. He seemed glad to hear that was my plan and offered his help.

For Daddy to offer to help me find a church in Colorado meant I would find a church in Colorado. He had been a Baptist minister in the state since the early 1950s, only a few years after the first Southern Baptists ventured into the state. He was well-known and highly respected by every Baptist leader and had served in several leadership positions himself. In his current position, he didn't serve as the pastor of a single church but worked with numerous churches covering half the state. All Daddy needed to do was announce that his son was ready to pastor a church and it would happen.

At the end of our conversation, Daddy said he would send a form for me to complete that he would share with churches seeking a pastor. Once I did that, he would get to work. He sent the form, and I filled it out as honestly and accurately as possible.

About a week and a half later, I received a letter from Daddy. He returned the form along with a handwritten letter explaining how he could not use the form because of the way I answered two of the questions. He also enclosed a small pamphlet that explained his position on the two issues.

I'll be honest, my initial reaction was anger. I knew when I answered the questions that Daddy would not agree with me. From prior conversations, both of us knew these were issues that led us to separate conclusions. The reason for my anger is that I considered the two issues insignificant. I was somewhat surprised the questions were even on his form. He was part of an old-school theology that was probably going to completely disappear with his generation. In addition, I was confident none of the churches he could recommend would have considered these were make-or-break matters.

The easy thing for me to do was to change my answers and resubmit the form. I couldn't do it. These weren't make-or-break issues for me or any church but being a man of honesty and integrity was. I couldn't lie in order to get a church. I called Daddy and told him that I couldn't change my answers. He replied that he couldn't help me unless I did.

Consequently, I never served as a pastor for a church in Colorado. Daddy didn't blackball me or throw up any roadblocks, he simply didn't help.

You might expect that Daddy and I both circled the wagons, got mad at one another, and never spoke to each other again. That didn't happen. What did happen is that our respect for one another increased. If Daddy had been willing to go against his own principles in order to benefit his son, I would have been disappointed. I never asked him, but I've also felt he would have been disappointed in me if I had lied on the form.

It took about a year and a half, but an opportunity to pastor a church in Texas appeared. As a quick aside, that was a reminder that my future was not dependent on Daddy working on my behalf—God was in control. He sent us to a church that needed someone like me. Despite the fact I was a city boy from a mountainous place, I was found by a small-town church on the flat plains of Texas and we worked well together for more than a dozen years.

During my time there, if I ever had a question about ministry, I called Daddy for his advice. He took great interest in my church and how it was doing. Whenever he came for a visit, I insisted that he preach in our church. When he retired, he moved to Texas and lived about 75 miles from where we lived and got to know our people well.

The lesson I gleaned from the experience is the importance of being true to your principles. Daddy didn't refuse to help me because he wanted me to fail or that he was teaching me a lesson. He refused to help me because he couldn't without violating his principles. He had turned down others who answered the questions as I had. It wasn't a matter of showing favoritism; it was a matter of integrity.

It's not surprising that we butted heads, and you might accuse both of us of being stubborn. I can be stubborn, but I hope remaining true to your principles is more than stubbornness.

My father and I were not the first to clash over principles. The prophet Jonah in the Old Testament provides an example of what happens when we hope to get God to change His principles. God assigned Jonah the task of preaching to the city of Nineveh. It was a city known for wickedness. It was a historical city to the east that served as a prosperous and powerful leader in the ancient world, known as a leading city of the Assyrian empire. As such, the people were considered wicked and godless by the Israelites.

When God instructed Jonah to preach to the Ninevites, it was to be a message of repentance. The possibility of repentance on the part of the enemies of God, caused Jonah to flee in the other direction. He hated the Ninevites and he knew God's character. He knew that if the people heeded the call to repentance, God would spare them from destruction (Jonah 4:2).

In his stubbornness, instead of heading east to Nineveh in obedience to God, he boarded a ship to the city of Tarshish, far to the west, in the opposite direction. He wanted nothing to do with God's plan because he knew God would remain true to His character.

You know the story of how God refused to allow Jonah to get away. He sent a storm to stop his travels, a group of frightened sailors to hurl him into the water, and a giant fish to bring him back to shore. Chastened, but still angry, Jonah went to Nineveh.

The city was so large that it took three days to walk from one end to the other. On the first day, still stubborn, Jonah did not preach a message of repentance. Instead, he preached a message of judgment— "Yet forty days and Nineveh will be overthrown" (Jonah 3:4). Although Jonah preached judgment, the people heard repentance, all of them, from the lowliest to the king. They repented with the hope that "God may turn and relent and withdraw His burning anger so that we will not perish" (Jonah 3:9).

True to His nature, "when God saw their deeds, that they turned from their wicked way," He responded with grace. God's actions are always consistent with His character. When God encounters genuine repentance, His response will be grace and forgiveness. To expect anything else means you do not know God.

I knew when I filled out Daddy's list of questions that he wouldn't like two of my answers. Perhaps I hoped he might overlook them, but that would have been disappointing in the long run. I wasn't surprised to receive his letter of rejection. There was a feeling of comfort and security, knowing that my father would always be who he said he was.

As I have shared this experience with friends over the years, many of them don't understand. They can't comprehend how we wouldn't make an exception for his son, someone he loved. Many others don't understand why I was not angry. I was dealing with a physical handicap that made it difficult for me to find a church, I should be able to at least count on my father to help, is the way they reason.

What they fail to understand is that Daddy did help. By teaching me such a great lesson about God, he provided truth that would carry me through many circumstances the remainder of my life. Faith is nothing more than believing God will be true to His character. I will say that teaching me the value of staying true to his principles was the greatest lesson Daddy ever taught. He revealed God. Since that time, I always tried to take God at His word.

Every morning, I ask God for my "daily bread." That's what Jesus taught us to pray, and I'm aware it means more than food in the pantry. Daily bread refers to whatever I need for the day. I might need a word of encouragement, a reminder of a bad attitude, a struggle to teach a lesson or anything else God knows I need. I'm able to offer that prayer in faith because God will be true to His character— "And my God will supply all your needs according to His riches in glory in Christ Jesus (Philippians 4:19).

Keep Loving People

The one who does not love does not know God, for God is love. (1 John 4:8)

For God so loved the world, that He gave His only begotten Son, that whoever believes in Him shall not perish, but have eternal life. (John 3:16)

"Teacher, which is the greatest commandment in the Law?" Jesus replied: "'Love the Lord your God with all your heart and with all your soul and with all your mind. This is the first and greatest commandment. And the second is like it: 'Love your neighbor as yourself.' All the Law and the Prophets hang on these two commandments." (Matthew 22:36-40)

Truth: The primary characteristic of God is love.

When Daddy retired, he and Mama left the beautiful city of Loveland, Colorado, and moved to the not-so-beautiful city of Amarillo, Texas. You might think it makes sense because a lot of folks move south for the warmer climate when they retire. However, Amarillo is not the desired location. When you throw in the wind, the Texas panhandle winters can be worse than Colorado. They chose that destination for a couple of reasons. They were both born and raised in the area, but more importantly, my maternal Grandmother needed closer attention and care in the final years of her life.

It was also good news for us. It meant they were now only ninety minutes away, and Amarillo was a place we often went for shopping or a doctor visit. Now we could include a visit to see Daddy and Mama. It didn't take long before Daddy introduced himself to pastors and church leaders and he was soon standing in a pulpit on most Sundays. He was especially effective during the interim time when a church is without a pastor. He had a knack for helping congregations move past any problems left behind by the former pastor and be prepared for a new pastor. His services were in high demand.

Watching him work with troubled churches was akin to watching a skilled athlete or musician. What he did, appeared to be effortless for him. But what he did was not the result of years of experience. Churches didn't respond to him because of what he did; they responded because of who he was.

The best way to explain it is to tell you about the only advice he ever gave me about being a pastor. Even though it was the only advice he ever offered, he did it more than one time. In fact, whenever I called and was struggling with a problem, his advice was always the same. It took some time, but I finally caught on and I quit calling for advice. I called for encouragement or just to hear a friendly voice, but I no longer needed his advice because it was always the same—keep loving the people.

For him, that was the essence of ministry.

He was correct—loving people is what it's all about. Everything else takes a backseat. The goal of ministry is not to build a church and then love the people. Neither is it to develop a powerful non-profit ministry and then love the people. Ministry is loving people—nothing more and nothing less.

Daddy exemplified this quality and people recognized it clearly. I have many friends on Facebook who attended Daddy's church when they were kids and many of them tell me how they loved my Dad. I know adults loved him. After my parents moved to Texas upon retirement, they frequently had people come visit who had been in a church where he was pastor years ago in Colorado. People all over Colorado and the Texas panhandle knew and loved Daddy, primarily because he first loved them.

He told me a story once of how this worked. He was interim pastor of a small church in Dumas, Texas, about

40 miles from where we lived. After a few weeks, he had the idea that they needed a choir for the Sunday morning service. He asked around to see if there was any interest and got a strange response from several people. Apparently, they had a choir in the past, but one particular lady sang so loud and off key that it made them sound horrible. They decided the best way to handle it was to disband the choir.

Daddy told them to organize the choir and he would take care of the offkey singer. Like always, he knew people and he had seen the woman in several situations. It was obvious that she was serious about prayer. He encouraged her as someone who cares enough to pray for people. Then he talked to her about people not having certain gifts, admitting that he liked to sing but wasn't a good singer. He then told her they were going to have a new choir and he wanted her to help. He asked if she would sit near the front and pray for the choir as they sang.

She was delighted. He realized that if her singing was that bad, it could not have been enjoyable for her. She simply saw it as a means to serve God. He provided a way for her to do what she wanted to do, serve God, which was beneficial to everyone. No one got their feelings hurt and everyone felt important. That's what loving other people accomplishes.

Teaching the importance of loving people is the best lesson Daddy could provide. If you attended church as a young child, the first Bible verse you learned was, "God so loved the world..." (John 3:16). The love of God is the primary theme running throughout the entire Bible. In the beginning, God expressed His love as He walked and talked with the first humans in the garden. The history of Israel recorded in the Old Testament is a tale of God's love for His chosen people. The ultimate expression of God's love was sending His "only begotten Son" to die so our sins can be forgiven. If you know anything about God at all then you know what it means to be loved.

If you do not know how to love, or if you are not loving toward others, then you don't know God. "The one who does not love does not know God, for God is love" (1 John 4:8). When you love someone, as you get to know them, you will discover that you begin to love the ones they love. This is commonly evident in healthy families. Because I love my wife, I also love her parents and siblings and extended family. I find myself wishing them well and concerned when they struggle.

This is the way it works with God. As we get to know Him, we begin to love those He loves. In that case, since He loves everybody, we find ourselves loving everyone. I'm not talking about some type of mushy, smarmy, hugging display of emotions. It is the kind of love that hopes and works for the best for others. Therefore, Jesus could speak of judgement on the basis of how we cared for others:

> *"Then the King will say to those on His right, 'Come, you who are blessed of My Father, inherit the kingdom prepared for you from the foundation of the world. For I was hungry, and you gave Me something to eat; I was thirsty, and you gave Me something to drink; I was a stranger, and you invited Me in; naked, and you clothed*

Me; I was sick, and you visited Me; I was in prison, and you came to Me.' Then the righteous will answer Him, 'Lord, when did we see You hungry, and feed You, or thirsty, and give You something to drink? And when did we see You a stranger, and invite You in, or naked, and clothe You? When did we see You sick, or in prison, and come to You?' The King will answer and say to them, 'Truly I say to you, to the extent that you did it to one of these brothers of Mine, even the least of them, you did it to Me.'" (Matthew 25:34-40)

Inheritance of the kingdom is determined by how we treat the hungry, thirsty, stranger, naked, sick, and prisoner. The reason these people are singled out is because the attitude we show toward them is genuine. He could have listed the wealthy, powerful, famous, and beautiful people of the world because they are to be loved as well. However, when it comes to those people, genuine love is not easily identified. It's likely that we treat them well, not because we love them, but because we want what they have. However, the way we treat the undesirable is a true indicator of our heart. We don't love them for what we can get. We love them because we love God who loves them.

The tendency to show preference to the wealthy revealed itself early in the history of Christianity. Even within the early church gatherings it was evident.

For if a man comes into your assembly with a gold ring and dressed in fine clothes, and there also comes in a poor man in dirty clothes, and you pay special attention to the one who is wearing the fine clothes, and say,

"You sit here in a good place," and you say to the poor man, "You stand over there, or sit down by my footstool," have you not made distinctions among yourselves, and become judges with evil motives? Listen, my beloved brethren: did not God choose the poor of this world to be rich in faith and heirs of the kingdom which He promised to those who love Him? (James 2:2-5)

God loves all people, rich and poor. However, he chooses the poor to demonstrate if our love is genuine. If we love Him, then we will love those He loves.

If you have more than one child, you know it is possible to love two different types of people equally. One might be neat, thrifty, obedient, and grateful, and the other might be sloppy, careless, reckless, and uncaring, but you love them both. The reason is because they are both your children. If you don't love them both, there is something wrong with you, not them.

No matter what kind of problem I was having at church, Daddy's advice was always, "Just love the people." Let me say, any problem you have at church is a people problem, there are no other kinds of church problems. The solution, to even the most cantankerous person, is to love them and treat them in a loving manner.

I watched Daddy do this over and over. He had numerous opportunities during his sixty years of ministry with churches. He was interim pastor at a church near our home in Texas but more than an hour and half from his house. He and Mama drove up on Saturday evenings, spent the evening in the community getting to know people. On Sunday, they were at church all day and then returned home late in the evening. On Wednesday, he returned for the afternoon and evening. Even when he was at home, miles away, he would be on the phone calling through the church directory, getting to know the people.

He had a special "trick" he did to remember people. During the phone conversation he focused on something unique they said. It might be "I work at the school cafeteria" or something he could associate with the name. Then he asked the person to introduce themselves to him at church next Sunday and mention they are the one who works at the school cafeteria. It encouraged people to come to church, greet him personally, and stimulate a conversation. It was genius and people discovered that he cared about them.

At this particular church, he arrived early one Wednesday afternoon and one of the church leaders pulled him aside into the church office. He said, "Bill, I need your resignation."

Daddy was stunned, but calmly replied, "You have it, but can I ask why?"

The man went on to explain that the church secretary had accused him of making inappropriate contact one day in the office. Daddy drove home, racking his brain trying to figure out what he had done. Daddy was friendly with everyone, including church secretaries, but no one who has ever known him would accuse him of such behavior. It was something completely out of left field.

After days of thinking, the only thing it could have possibly been was in the office one day, the secretary wanted him to look at a chart on her computer screen. The numbers were small, and he had to lean over to get a closer view. In doing so, remember his balance was always precarious because of the wooden leg, he braced himself on the back of her chair and perhaps his arm brushed against her shoulder.

He also knew this secretary was especially close to the previous pastor. After Daddy came to the church, the attendance increased, offerings were high, new people were joining, and many people were returning to the fold. He suspected she was jealous of what was happening.

Daddy went out of his way to avoid talking about the issue to anyone at the church. Once it was apparent that he was gone, people called him, drove the 100 miles to his house to talk to him, and wrote letters, but he never accused or blamed anyone. He always spoke highly of everyone involved and encouraged them to stay faithful. When you love people, it sometimes means you turn the other cheek. His sole purpose was to do everything he could to help the church, even if it meant not defending himself.

I wasn't quite so magnanimous. I personally knew the church leader who asked Daddy for his resignation and sent him a scathing letter. I'm sure it didn't do any good, and I hope it didn't cause any harm. It did make me feel better at the time, but I'm sure it wasn't done out of love. I still had much to learn.

Loving other people is seldom easy. Especially when you consider the people Jesus specifically reminded us to love. The poor and destitute top the list. But remember,

God loves all people and if we know Him, then we will love all people as well.

One day, Jesus was questioned about securing eternal life. He assured the questioner that it was a result of loving God and loving your neighbor. The lawyer asking the question pressed the matter and wanted to know the identity of this neighbor. He wanted to limit the pool of people he was required to love. To be honest, most of us would have asked the same thing. We don't mind loving certain people, but typically the ones who are easier to love. Again, God loves all people.

Jesus' response to the man's question was to tell the story of the Good Samaritan. You remember the story—a man was beaten, robbed, and left to die on the side of the road. Two religious people came by and ignored the man because they had religious things to do. Then a Samaritan, an outcast himself, came upon the man. He stopped, took him to town and paid for his care to get back on his feet.

Jesus used the story to identify the neighbor to be loved. Our neighbor is anyone who comes along with a need. We are to love them just as we would a family member or a close friend.

Daddy continually demonstrated what it meant to love people. Not only those within the church, but it included people wherever he went. I remember as a kid, we would go into a restaurant for a meal, and before we left, Daddy visited with everyone there and treated them like they were friends. When he and Mama got older, they frequently ate dinner at an IHOP in their neighborhood. When he was there, the staff treated him like family. He knew about their personal lives. He prayed for them and asked about things they had previously shared with him.

The interesting thing is that Daddy was not naturally a people person. He told me that when he was young, if he saw an acquaintance coming down the street, he would cross to the other side to avoid talking with them. He naturally preferred to be alone with his thoughts. He had to learn how to love others because that's what people who love God do. There was nothing phony about him either, his love for others was genuine. That's how people are when they know God.

The principal Catholic church in San Francisco made the news a few years back, and not for good reasons. There are several recessed entrances to the church building that serve as frequent sleeping quarters for the homeless. In order to keep the homeless away from the building, the church installed a watering system in each sheltered alcove. Throughout the night, water comes pouring down, soaking anyone who might be seeking shelter from the church, and driving away the unwanted homeless.

In contrast, Pope Francis had showers installed for the homeless under St. Peter's portico. Following his example, ten other parishes in Rome chose to do the same thing for the homeless in their part of the city. It all started when an emissary of the Pope actually took the time to get to know a homeless man, Franco. He listened when Franco told him that food was readily available throughout the city, but what the homeless really need was a place to clean up.

It seems to make sense that everybody is loved by somebody. Even the most despised, despicable, detestable person in the world has someone in their life who loves (or perhaps loved) them. Who is the most unlovable person you can imagine? Perhaps it is Adolf Hitler or Charles Manson. It might even be someone you know, an individual who treated you cruelly, or harmed you in some awful way. Heaven forbid, it might be a person who caused the death of one of your loved ones or ruined your life in some other way.

My point is that even that person, the one you consider most unlovable, is loved by someone. They might not have a lot of people who care for them, and perhaps they have never felt loved, but at some point in their life, I think it is safe to say that everyone has been loved.

Stick with me for a few more paragraphs because I am going to make a significant point that will apply to you.

I am going to suggest that it is likely that the person who loves the unlovable person is also the person who knows them the best. Perhaps it's a mother, spouse, father, child, or close friend. It's almost always true that people who love us the most are also the ones who know us the best.

That is especially true in my life. The one person who knows me better than any other person alive is my wife Sharon. She is also the person who loves me more than anyone else loves me. My life is filled with people who love me (I am most fortunate), but it is the one who knows me best who also loves me most.

I suspect the same is also true for you. The ones who love you most are not casual acquaintances. They are the ones who live with you day after day and know the most about your ways. They know your failures and weaknesses more than others. They know what makes you angry and unreasonable. They have seen you act out, and they have been there when you embarrassed everyone in the room.

When you put all of this together, the conclusion I come to is that the key to loving another person is to get to know them. The more you know them the more you will love them.

Perhaps the reason God loves us so much is because He knows us so well. He knows why we do the things we do. He knows our fears and weaknesses. He knows our worst sins and failures. Because He knows us, He loves us.

That's why Daddy talked to the stranger on the street, the waitress at the IHOP, the people in the church. He wanted to know them so he could love them. This is what God does and what God's people do.

Always Trust God

Now faith is the assurance of things hoped for, the conviction of things not seen. (Hebrews 11:1)

...for we walk by faith, not by sight. (2 Corinthians 5:7)

Truth: Faith is the greatest gift from God.

In 1943, when Daddy was 18 years old, World War II was raging, both in Europe and the Pacific. Young men were needed for battle. On his birthday, he was drafted by the Marines, shipped off to training camp, and then about two months later, literally shipped off to the far side of the Pacific Ocean. He was one of the thousands of Marines who flooded the beaches of the volcanic island of Iwo Jima that served as an airbase and outpost for the Japanese.

I remember how he described the ground on the island as being hot enough that they slept on top of their bedding. It was almost nighttime one evening when he, and 14 other Marines, were bedding down for the night behind a hill. A mortar shell landed nearby, and scattered mortar fragments into his right leg and a knuckle on his left hand. Daddy and one other Marine were the only two carried away alive, and the other survivor died later that night.

His next stop was in a hospital tent on Guam, another Pacific island. His injured leg was put in traction, and maggots were placed on the wound to eat out the infection. Eventually, the leg was casted, and he was sent to the Naval hospital at Pearl Harbor. While at that hospital, his entire body was encased in plaster from his shoulders, down over his hips, fully covering the broken leg and to the knee on the other leg. When he saw me in the hospital years later, it must have reminded him of his own experience.

Two months after being wounded, Daddy arrived back in the States. For the next three and a half years (yes, I mean years) he was in the hospital, undergoing numerous surgeries and treatments to preserve his leg. He eventually left the hospital against medical advice. The bone in his right leg refused to grow back together. He finally received a letter indicating that if he did not return to the hospital, they would stop paying his medical expenses. When he returned, the only course of action was to amputate his right leg.

As a 23-year-old man, he had to find a way to provide for himself and my mother (they were married while he was in the hospital). He went to school and secured work as a bookkeeper. They were even able to purchase a house. It appeared life was finally going in the right direction.

One Saturday afternoon, Daddy was driving down a city street and noticed a girl standing off to the side with a bag of clothes over her shoulder, waiting for the car to pass. Just as Daddy's car reached the pedestrian, a five-year-old girl stepped out from behind the bag of clothes and walked right in front of his car. There was no way he could avoid impact. Mama described how she could never forget the sight of Daddy holding the lifeless body of that little girl.

That should have been enough—but it wasn't. About two months later, my sister was born. When Linda was only three days old, while Mama was still in the hospital, the worst tornado in the history of the city struck and took a hard swipe at their new house. All the windows were broken, everything inside, even the interior of cabinets and drawers, was covered with mud. All the furniture was ruined, and the siding was torn from the house.

I wonder if he was beginning to feel like Job at this point, but there was still more to come. I was born 18 months after my sister. By that time, Daddy had moved his family to Brownwood, Texas, to enroll in school and pursue a call to the ministry. One Sunday afternoon, he took the family to Brownwood Lake for a picnic. My mother put me in the shallow water of the lake and let me splash around. Two weeks later, I had a fever and was eventually diagnosed with polio.

A new adventure of moving from hospital to hospital for treatment and then therapy. Obviously, I survived, but with severe limitations in the use of my arms and legs. Consequently, Daddy's world was now cluttered with leg braces, wheelchairs, doctor visits, and all the worries that come with having an unhealthy child. To make matters worse, while they were in Fort Worth with me in the hospital, he had problems finding a place to live. At that time, everyone was afraid of polio, and whenever people discovered he had a son in the hospital with the infection, they were forced to leave their apartment. Daddy explained that as soon as he got my mother and sister situated in a new place, he would start looking for the next apartment.

Stepping back and looking at the time frame of his life, from his 18th birthday until his 26th birthday, eight years later, it was stunning. He went through war, seeing friends die and killing the enemy, losing his leg after three and a half years in the hospital, accidentally killing a five-year-old girl, his house destroyed by a tornado, and an infant son struggle to survive a crippling disease.

What does a man learn from that?

As far back as I can remember, whenever I faced a difficult obstacle, Daddy's recommendation was to trust God. This was the advice from a man who had been through the fire, staring death and destruction in the face numerous times. He always lived by that advice. Several times as I was growing up and struggling with my own frustrations about being crippled, I asked Daddy if he wished he had his leg back. He never complained, but I knew it made his life harder. He frequently had what are called "phantom pains" in his leg that was not there. He talked about wanting to grab his foot because it hurt so much, but there was no foot. There was nothing he could do other than tolerate the pain for a few hours. His life was not easy.

Yet, when I asked him if he wished for his leg, he always said, "No."

I struggled with understanding because nearly every morning, as I strapped on my leg braces before putting on my pants, I wished I didn't have to do it. I wanted to be able to get up out of bed and get dressed like everyone else. I wanted to run around the yard and play ball. Truthfully, I think I was ten years old before it dawned on me that I would never play first base for the Yankees. Somewhere in the back of my mind, I thought I would wake up one day and everything would be fine.

When Daddy said he never wished that he had his leg back, I didn't understand. The reason for my lack of understanding is that I had not yet learned all the things he had learned. School was still in session for me.

Day after day, I watched Daddy handle his physical disability as if it wasn't even there. In fact, more than one friend was surprised to learn that he had an artificial leg because they never saw any evidence. He showed me the power of accepting that God gives us what we need, even if it doesn't make sense. That is the essence of faith.

I have always been a bookworm, and there was a time when Daddy kept an office in our basement at the house. He had shelves filled with books, and I could always find something to read. I discovered theology, Baptist history, sermon writing, Bible studies, and everything else suitable for a Christian library. It was during that time that I decided I was going to write a book someday. In fact, I decided that my book would be about faith.

What you're reading now is the 26th book that I have written, and I have yet to address the subject of faith. It's not from a lack of thought of trying. I have spent hours pondering the concept and striving to understand it in a way that I can communicate to someone else, and I always get lost in the depth of the subject.

Anything you say about faith must begin with Hebrews 11:1 – "Now faith is the assurance of things hoped for, the conviction of things not seen." This is the Bible's definition of faith. Faith is the "conviction" of what we can't see. The word can also be understood as "evidence." When it speaks of "things not seen," we immediately think of God. I've never seen God, yet I believe He exists. How? I have evidence. That evidence is not a photograph or a video or DNA. The evidence I have that God exists is faith.

The first part of the phrase speaks of things "hoped for." What are the things I hope for? Life, love, provisions. The "assurance" that I will have these things is faith. My hope is not based on my latest doctor's report, how others have treated me, or what I can find in the pantry. I'm assured of these things because of faith.

Faith is the glue of life. It holds everything together. It is faith that binds me together with God. It is also faith that holds me in the proper place in the world. I have confidence that everything I need in this life will come to me because I have faith. Essentially, everything I need in this life and the next life, in the physical world and the spiritual world, is available through faith.

The eleventh chapter of Hebrews, after providing this definition of faith, dives headlong into a list of great men and women of faith who have proven this definition is correct. It was faith that made Abel's sacrifice acceptable to God. It was faith that allowed Enoch to bypass death and go straight to God. It was faith that led Noah to do one of the craziest things any man has ever done, built a huge boat on dry land. It was faith that drove Abraham to a foreign land where he found his authentic inheritance—an entire nation.

The author of Hebrews goes on and on, depicting all the heroes of Israel and how their faith made them unique and made their lives possible. These people all had faith, but then he says, "God provided something better for us..."

(Hebrews 11:40). Not only do we have faith and the witness of these great men and women of faith, but also, we have Jesus, "the author and perfecter of faith..." (Hebrews 12:2). If I may continue with my analogy of faith being the glue of life, I would say that now, since Jesus showed up, faith is the "superglue" of life.

My son does a lot of bodywork on cars. He's been doing it for years, and in his shop, you will discover nearly any tool or device you will ever need to repair a car. He has some amazing glue that I've seen him use a few times. When he applies this glue, whatever it sticks together is permanent. I recently had him use his glue to repair a part on my wheelchair. A clip holding a cable in place was broken, and I needed it fixed so the cable didn't bend. He brought his glue gun to the house and made quick work of my project.

The glue is made of two chemicals. When they are separate, neither one is sticky. The magic happens when they come together. That's when they form an unbreakable bond. The glue gun has a unique nozzle that mixes the chemicals together as they are applied to the surface. It only takes a few minutes to see that when they are combined, the glued objects are now permanently attached. I have no reason to doubt the clip that holds the cable on my chair will be in place long after I'm gone.

Faith, like my son's superglue, has two elements. First, there is the faith that comes from God. We've already seen Hebrews 12:2 that identifies Jesus as the "author" of faith. Speaking about our life before Christ, Paul reminds us that we were dead, living in lusts and indulging the desires of the flesh (Ephesians 2:1-3). But God changed us and brought us back to life. He did this, not because we deserved it, but out of His grace. This gift of grace came to us through faith, which is identified as "the gift of God" (Ephesians 2:8-9).

The second element is the faith we provide. When Jesus was sleeping in the boat on the stormy Sea of Galilee, the disciples panicked and woke him up. His response, after calming the storm, was to ask, "Do you still have no faith?" (Mark 4:40). A Roman officer begged Jesus to heal his servant, suggesting that all that was necessary was to say the word. Jesus' response was, "I have not found anyone in Israel with such great faith" (Matthew 8:10). Remember the woman with the bleeding issue who reached through the crowd to touch Jesus. His statement to her was that "your faith has made you well..." (Mark 5:34). Or, who can forget the Canaanite woman whose persistent pleading encouraged Jesus to heal her daughter? Jesus told her, "your faith is great" (Matthew 15:28).

It seems that although faith is a gift from God, it must also be exercised and used by us. God provides faith; it's a gift. However, we can't stick it in our back pocket and save it for some time in the future or hope it's enough to get us into heaven. To experience the benefits and blessings of faith, we must exercise that faith. Like my son's superglue, God's gift and our usage combine to become the glue that not only attaches us to God but also connects us to the world around us.

What we often fail to understand is that faith is not a substance; it is an action, an activity. The disciples in the boat panicked and Jesus asked, "Where is your faith." The Roman commander, the bleeding woman, and the mother of the sick child all acted, they found Jesus, then asked, expecting Him to help, and He praised their faith. Faith is the evidence of things not seen (Hebrews 11:1), so it allows us to believe God even when our eyes and other senses say otherwise. The only evidence the Roman commander had that Jesus could heal his daughter simply by saying the word was his faith. The bleeding woman fought through the crowd to touch Jesus, not because a doctor suggested it, but because her faith compelled her.

As he worked his way through storm after storm, Daddy showed me how to utilize faith in God as a means of dealing with every situation of life. Time after time, as I saw God remain faithful to Daddy, it was easy to realize God would be faithful to me as well. Whenever I heard Daddy tell me to keep trusting God, it became easier and easier for me to do the same.

To believe God is enough for everything we need is not an easy lesson to learn. Even though I had the advantage of watching Daddy live out that truth, I had to go through my own crucible.

When I announced I was leaving to go to college to pursue God's call to preach, my friends were excited. A few of them, who loved me greatly, believed God was going to heal me and allow me to walk, so I could obediently follow His calling. It made sense to them and me, so we all began to pray. There was an enormous amount of earnest prayer invested in healing happening.

One evening we were gathered in the prayer room at a friend's house. I was seated in a chair in the middle of the room, and several encircled me and prayed. All of us anticipated we would see a miracle that evening. I can truthfully say, I mustered up as much faith as I possibly could that night and attempted to rise from the chair and stand. I immediately fell to the floor. Nothing happened.

At least nothing happened physically. I left that room, knowing that physical healing was not going to happen for me. My life changed in the room in that I finally realized what Daddy had been showing me—faith in God is always enough. I didn't need two strong legs to be a preacher. It wasn't necessary for me to be physically fit to do what God called me to do. I knew from that moment that God would always provide whatever I needed.

God has always been there for me; He has never failed.

In our first year of marriage, we were given two days' notice that we had to move out of an apartment we planned to be in for two more months. The next day, a friend offered to let us have his whole house for free. God was there.

When Sharon had to have an emergency c-section with our first child, and we were a thousand miles away from family, God took care of us.

When two-year-old Matthew was bitten by a rattlesnake in our front yard, neighbors just happened to be in our house, and God used them to take care of us and get us to the doctor 30 miles away.

When Andrew, at one-month of age, was put in the hospital for meningitis, God was there for us, and he recovered completely.

When Sharon had cancer as a young woman, even though I only had enough faith to ask for ten more years, God has since given us 35 and still counting.

When we left a church after serving for 13 years as pastor with no place to go, God provided. On the very first Sunday after relocating, we found the church that loved us, adopted us, and healed us.

When working a job that did pay enough to meet our expenses, God provided a ministry job that opened opportunities for years to come.

It's impossible to recall the number of times when we had a financial need, and God was there, sending a generous person to provide.

Without fail, whenever I have exercised faith, God has been faithful to take care of me. His provision was not always what I asked for or expected, and occasionally His provision led me to another challenge, but He has also been my greatest friend and best resource. Amazingly, His gifts have also come before I even recognized I had a need at times.

Many years ago, while I was the pastor of a small rural church, Sharon and I planned to attend a denominational convention in Dallas. I knew Dallas was a big city and expected the convention center to be a large place, but we weren't worried. We were accustomed to Sharon, dropping me off at the front door before parking the car. I could walk in from there on my crutches. What I didn't realize was how large the convention center was and how dumb an idea of dropping someone off at the front door was as well.

About a month before the scheduled convention, a young man in our church told me about a mutual acquaintance who had been injured in a farming accident years ago and used a wheelchair fulltime. He told me about an electric chair the man was using and that he was selling them as well. He wanted me to visit with him and see for myself. I didn't think much about it at the time. Ever since I was a kid, I wanted an electric wheelchair, but I knew they were far too expensive.

About three weeks went by, and the young man caught me at church and asked if I had ever gone out to visit the man and seen the chair. I could tell it was important to him for some reason, so I assured him I would make the trip. Early the next week, I went to the man's farm, and he was expecting me. He took me out to his barn and demonstrated the electric chair. It was great, and I was a little jealous.

He then asked if I would like to have one. I replied that I would love one, but there was no way I could afford to buy one. Without a moment's hesitation, he said, it's already been paid for if you want it. The young man from church and his father made the arrangements. It goes without saying that I was shocked and surprised. Yes, I wanted it.

Without knowing it, I needed the chair. Upon approaching the Dallas Convention Center, it was obvious the electric wheelchair was a necessity. Without it, we would have simply turned around and driven home. In that particular instance, God knew my need long before I did. I had faith I could manage the logistics of the convention, but I had no idea how God would provide.

I'm still learning the lesson, but I do understand how Daddy could say it didn't matter if he had his leg or not. I'm fine living out my days in a wheelchair. It can be hard most of the time, but God has always provided. Between the faith He has given and the faith I exercise, we are superglued together and prepared to take on whatever challenge comes along. That is one of the most valuable things I know about my heavenly father, as taught to me by my earthly father.

Overcoming Obstacles

But David said to Saul, "Your servant was tending his father's sheep. When a lion or a bear came and took a lamb from the flock, I went out after him and attacked him, and rescued it from his mouth; and when he rose up against me, I seized him by his beard and struck him and killed him. Your servant has killed both the lion and the bear; and this uncircumcised Philistine will be like one of them, since he has taunted the armies of the living God." And David said, "The Lord who delivered me from the paw of the lion and from the paw of the bear, He will deliver me from the hand of this Philistine." And Saul said to David, "Go, and may the Lord be with you." (1 Samuel 17:34-37)

Truth: God uses obstacles to stretch our faith.

As I've clearly described in the preceding chapters, when I was 11 months and two weeks old, a large brick wall was placed directly in front of my face. Just two weeks shy of my first birthday, I came down with polio. From that moment on, every physical activity became a challenge. At first, there was some concern if I would survive the initial illness. When it became apparent that I would live, the prognosis was that I would never walk.

Starting school in first grade was a major step because the school was not prepared for a wheelchair student. From first grade, all the way through seminary, it was a significant ordeal when I went to a new school. Often, they would discourage me; always, they would have to make special arrangements.

In school, when I wanted to play the trumpet in the band, they thought it would be impossible. Every new place I went to was an obstacle to overcome because they had never had someone in a wheelchair before.

At the age of 21, when God called me to preach, some of my closest friends thought it meant that God was going to heal me since I was not physically able to pastor. In college, the Chairman of the Religion Department told me that I would probably never be able to pastor a church.

At seminary, they encouraged me to skip preaching and study for a counseling position.

When it was time to move on after serving my first church for 13 years, there was no place to go because no other church was interested. Even now, in a much friendlier world, when I travel, I often encounter enormous obstacles–buildings and bathrooms that are inaccessible, ill-equipped hotel rooms, and airlines that are virtually impossible without direct help.

I don't tell you my story to win your sympathy. In fact, those who know me will tell you that the last thing I want is sympathy. I tell you my story because it is also your story. All of us face obstacles in life. Many of mine are physical and visible, like a flight of stairs. Your obstacles may not be as evident, but they are just as real.

Obstacles are a normal part of life. Successful people have learned how to deal with obstacles. Unsuccessful people allow the obstacle to keep them from accomplishing their goal.

I recently saw a news story about a young woman who had been on unemployment, but her benefits ran out, so she was left without any help. The purpose of the time limit for benefits was to encourage people to find jobs. When she was asked why she did not have a job, she replied that she could not find one that provided good health insurance, paid vacations, and enough time off. Her response was just to quit looking, and now she was left with nothing. Her obstacle was that there was not a job that she wanted. For whatever reason, she chose lie down in front of her obstacle and give up.

Daddy was great at dealing with obstacles, and he had his share. He was unable to complete his college education because of a young family and a crippled baby. It would have been easy to go back to Amarillo and return to his bookkeeping job and earn a decent living for his family.

One of the reasons he began his ministry in Colorado was because of his lack of a college degree. I hate to say it, but preachers have always been a dime a dozen in Texas, especially Baptist ones. Without a college degree, you become the low man on the list. Even later in life, after he had established himself, lack of a degree was an occasional obstacle because he was working in a professional field.

Consequently, Daddy went to Colorado, where Baptist preachers were scarce, and his ministry flourished. His first church was in a small farming town in southeastern Colorado, still recovering from the remnants of the dust bowl days. Because the pay was low, he bought a shoe repair shop to earn a little extra money. Even though he had no idea how to repair shoes, he bragged that he only ruined one pair.

From this town on the plains, he moved his family to the mountains and a church in one of the coldest spots in the state. The church had a tiny building, a log cabin of no more than 200 square feet. Everyone squeezed in, but Sunday School classes gathered in cars in the parking lot. Within a short time, Daddy led the church to construct an actual church building. Even though he had little ability as a carpenter, he did much of the labor himself. That church building stood for many years.

His next church was finally in an actual city, Colorado Springs, to be precise. It was not sprawling with newcomers like it is now, but it was far better than where we had been. Our house was next door to the church on the last street on the east side of town. Many years after we left, Daddy was invited back to speak at an anniversary celebration. While he was there, they presented him with a check. Apparently, they discovered that years earlier, when he was the pastor, the church missed paying his salary several times, and they wanted to make it up. Daddy graciously thanked them but added he could have used the money a lot more back then.

One piece of advice Daddy gave me about being a pastor is that I will never be rich, and especially don't expect to make anything from doing funerals and weddings. He was correct, and it's probably accurate that I lost money doing funerals and weddings. In fact, I had to borrow money at a funeral once, but that's a story for another day.

The point of recounting this bit of history is to say that Daddy never allowed obstacles to make him a failure. He didn't always succeed, but he never gave up. It might have been a physical struggle, a family matter, a financial need, or whatever; he didn't judge life based on successes and failures.

The story of David and Goliath is about overcoming obstacles. Because this story is popular among children, we run the risk of relegating it to the preschool department and neglecting it as adults. The danger is that we might conclude the familiar story has nothing new to teach us as adults. However, the encounter between the shepherd boy David and the giant warrior Goliath reveals some essential truths that we really cannot understand until we become adults. Therefore, it is a great teacher for all ages.

The key to success is to learn to turn obstacles into opportunities. We will never be totally free of obstructions or problems. Those who are successful are the ones who have learned how to make something positive out of something negative.

When we consider an obstacle, there are different approaches we can take. These options are revealed with the various characters in the story of David and Goliath.

FEAR - Saul

The fight against Goliath should have belonged to Saul. He was the strongest and most impressive of the Israelites. The challenge was his. However, for 40 days (1 Samuel 17:16), he listened to the challenges and taunts of Goliath and cowered in fear inside his tent. Saul represents a common approach to an obstacle—hide from the challenge or ignore the problem. He was not on the front lines where a leader should be. The reason is that he didn't want to face the problem. A lack of faith causes fear like this.

Rather than accepting the challenge and leading the nation, Saul's solution was to offer a big reward for someone else to step up and face the obstacle (see 1 Samuel 17:25). Those who are successful don't sit back and wait for someone else to clear the way. It has often been said that fear is the opposite of faith. Because of Saul's lack of faith, he was gripped by fear, and the challenge was too great for him.

FACADE - Israelite Army

Every morning, the army would dress up in battle array and shout a war cry (see 1 Samuel 17:20). They even marched to the battlefield and stood opposite the Philistines (v.21). However, they never confronted the enemy. Each day they turned and fled (v.24). That must have been a sight straight out of a Monty Python movie.

We do this sometimes when we just "grin and bear it." People have obstacles, and often they just live as if it is not there— "if I ignore it, perhaps it will go away." This is a kind of magical thinking, but it does nothing to solve the problem. We don't overcome obstacles by pretending they don't exist.

FAITH - David

The third response to an obstacle in our story is the one demonstrated by the shepherd boy, David. He shows us how faith handles obstacles. It begins by recognizing the possibility that obstacles can become opportunities. The goal of an obstacle is to cause us to quit, to give up without a struggle. If we do not strive to overcome an obstacle, we will always fail. It was Hockey legend, Wayne Gretzky, who said, "You miss 100% of shots you don't take."

Goliath's goal was to get the army of God's people to turn and run. The difference between David and Saul's army was that David did not see the obstacle; he saw an opportunity. Instead of fearing failure, he saw the possibility of victory. "Let no man's heart fail on account of him (Goliath); your servant will go and fight with this Philistine" (1 Samuel 17:32).

Once he determined to confront the obstacle, David teaches us that we must not focus on the obstacle. Imagine the size of Goliath in comparison to David. The young shepherd was so small that he could not even wear Saul's armor. It would be like me standing up against Shaquille O'Neal. It would have been easy for David to have been so blinded by the enormity of the enemy that he could not see anything else.

However, notice that David did not cower in fear. Listen to what he said to Goliath: "This day the Lord will deliver you up into my hands, and I will strike you down and remove your head from you. And I will give the dead bodies of the army of the Philistines this day to the birds of the sky and the wild beasts of the earth, that all the earth may know that there is a God in Israel, and that all this assembly may know that the Lord does not deliver by sword or by spear; for the battle is the Lord's and He will give you into our hands" (1 Samuel 17:46-47). He did not see Goliath; he saw God.

Recently, on the Facebook page of my old High School, there was a notice that my Driver's Education teacher died. It brought back a lot of memories because taking the class was a challenge. I could not drive a car unless it had hand controls, so when he had a free period, Mr. Weigand would take me to my house, and we would drive our car that was properly equipped. I know it must have been nerve-wracking for him since the car didn't have the customary brake pedal in front of the passenger's seat.

I passed and got my license, but I remember a tendency that needed to be corrected. I found myself driving in the direction I was looking. If I looked at the side mirror too long, I would swerve to that side. It seems that I always went in the direction I was looking.

That's true with most of life. Whatever has the focus of our attention is what controls our destiny. If we focus on the obstacle, the destiny will always be struggle and failure. Saul and his army were consumed with the taunting giant, so they were paralyzed with fear. David came along, and he wasn't focused on the obstacle. Instead, he saw an opportunity. In order to be successful, we must have an objective that commands our attention. David's objective was to glorify God, regardless of the opposition.

Even though David stepped forward to fight for Israel, not everyone was supportive of his bravery. Saul's response to David was not encouraging: "You are not able to go against this Philistine to fight with him; for you are but a youth while he has been a warrior from his youth" (1 Samuel 17:33).

The old comic strip "Shoe" often takes a swipe at social and political issues as well as the everyday decisions of life. In one strip, the title character "Shoe" was sitting on a barstool moaning that "when I finished high school, I wanted to join the military, but everyone said wait. Then

I wanted to go to law school, but they said wait. Then I wanted to get married, and they said wait. Finally, I wanted to start my own businesses but again they said wait.

"So, what did you do?"

"What else, I became a waiter."

Whenever you attempt to do something for God, anticipate opposition. People will discourage and distract you. Sometimes, it is those closest to you. When discouragement comes from people who care about you, it's especially tough. Daddy never tried to dissuade me from doing anything. He was my biggest cheerleader.

I needed it because my mother was super cautious. I often felt like she wanted me to stay at home and be safe. When I was young and began walking on crutches, Mama often walked beside me with a finger hooked on a belt loop of my pants. It was her way of being prepared. She continued doing it even as I got older, and we began to tease her that if I fell, she would either rip my pants off or fall down with me. It was her way of keeping me safe.

But Daddy was at the bottom of the ledge, encouraging me to fall into his arms. He had overcome so many obstacles in his life that he convinced me I could do the same thing. He also assured me that I not only had his help but, more importantly, God's help.

One of David's most exceptional qualities was his confidence in God. He recalled how God was there when he was threatened by a lion and a bear while tending his father's sheep. "The Lord who delivered me from the paw of the lion and from the paw of the bear, He will deliver me from the hand of this Philistine" (1 Samuel 17:37). His faith was based on his knowledge of God and his experience with God. He knew that God could win this battle. A giant Philistine was no match for God. David anticipated success.

But you might say this was no mere animal. "...Goliath, from Gath, whose height was six cubits and a span (over 9 feet). And he had a bronze helmet on his head, and he was clothed with scale-armor which weighed five thousand shekels of bronze... And the shaft of his spear was like a weaver's beam, and the head of his spear weighed six hundred shekels of iron..." (1 Samuel 17:4-7).

The easiest thing for David to do when he saw the situation, would have been to excuse himself and go back home. No one would have blamed him if he headed back to his father's sheep.

When I was being considered for a fulltime position as a consultant with Texas Baptists, the man who was hiring called to ask my father if he thought I could do the job. It required significant travel and time away from home, and he wasn't sure I was physically up to the challenge. Daddy never said anything to me about the call, but the man who hired me told me that Daddy assured him I could do whatever I set my mind to do. He knew it was true because he had done it many times himself.

One of our boys was playing Little League baseball, and of course, he was the best player on the team. It was a late Saturday afternoon game, and the score was tight as the game entered the final innings. The other team was batting, and we needed to keep them from scoring. With a runner on second, the batter hit a line drive to right field. All the fans of the other team began to cheer, and everyone on our side groaned. Right field is where you always put the kid who can't catch and seldom pays attention.

However, this time it was different. The kid ran straight to the ball, picked it up without hesitation, and like a pro, threw the ball hard toward the Catcher. It was apparent there was going to be a close play as the runner rounded third base. Our fans were feeling much better. Our Catcher, who actually was the best player on our team, would make the play and save the game. He was all set to catch the ball and apply the tag. The ball came on target and arrived just as the runner began to slide. Dust flew, and all the fans were silent for a split second.

Breaking the silence was the cry of the Umpire, "He's safe!"

One side cheered, and our side groaned. When the dust cleared, it was apparent the ball rolled up to the backstop as the Catcher failed to make the catch. With a heartbroken expression on his face, the Catcher looked at the Coach and said, "The sun was in my eyes."

He was correct. It was late afternoon, and looking toward right field meant he had to gaze directly into the sun. He was correct; the sun was in his eyes. However, all of us knew it didn't make any difference. They were not going to replay anything, and being blinded by the sun was not an excuse.

Immediately upon hearing the Catcher make an excuse, I thought about my High School band teacher, Mr. Preizner. Like any good music teacher, he was tough and demanding. There was a large banner hanging in the front of the music room where the band rehearsed. During practice, whenever Mr. Preizner heard a mistake, he would immediately wave his hands, indicating that everyone should stop.

When the band was silent, Mr. Preizner would stand at the front of the room and scowl at the band member who played the clunker. Nobody wanted to be the target of his fearsome scowl. If the clunker was especially offensive, he would walk over and stand directly in front of the offender. The bad musician was likely to begin making excuses— "I had too much homework and didn't have time to practice," or "My parents told me I was making too much noise." As everyone in the room waited silently out of fear, Mr. Preizner would take his baton and slowly point to the banner hanging in the front of the room.

The banner contained only three words— "Results, not excuses!"

Those three words have stuck with me for my entire life. They are consistent with how David approached Goliath. They are also consistent with what my father taught me.

The Church is Worthy of Sacrifice

Husbands, love your wives, just as Christ also loved the church and gave Himself up for her, so that He might sanctify her, having cleansed her by the washing of water with the word, that He might present to Himself the church in all her glory, having no spot or wrinkle or any such thing; but that she would be holy and blameless. (Ephesians 5:25-27)

But even if I am being poured out as a drink offering upon the sacrifice and service of your faith, I rejoice and share my joy with you all. (Philippians 2:17)

Truth: God loves the church and gave His life for His church.

Daddy told me that when he and Mama got married, they had an agreement. It sounds rather harsh in today's world, but understand, this was 1945, and times were much different. They agreed that Daddy would provide for the family, and Mama would raise the kids. They did that, and both did an excellent job.

Mama was the ideal mother, June Cleaver had nothing on her. She provided every physical need we had. It was always comforting to know that if anything ever happened, we could always get in touch with Mama. She wasn't off to work somewhere; she was at home. Food was always on the table, clothes were washed and ironed, and any other preparations necessary were handled as well.

Daddy fulfilled his part. He didn't make much money, but we never felt like we had to do without anything. It was a simple world. He worked hard, and his days were long. From as early as I can remember, he was a preacher, which was his primary source of income. He also received a disability check from Uncle Sam every month and occasionally worked odd jobs, but he depended on the church to provide most of our needs.

Even though the pay was not much, Daddy took his work with the church seriously. He worked long hours. He left the house after breakfast, came home for lunch and was there most evenings for dinner, but left soon after the evening meal, either for church meetings or visitation. He usually took most of Saturday off, but Sunday was always a hard, grueling day. He poured himself into his work for the church. Consequently, his love for the church became intense.

Somehow, he taught me to love the church, as well. I was not what some think is the typical preacher's kid. I never had a period in my life, even as a rebellious teen, when I quit the church. I didn't mind attending twice on Sunday and every Wednesday night, and occasionally other times set aside for special events. My friends were at church. I remember always being comfortable at church.

Because Daddy poured his life and work into the church, it was hard to watch him in the final years when he could no longer do so. When his work ended in an official capacity, he continued to serve the church as an interim pastor. By this time, he had moved to Texas and had to start from scratch. All his previous ministry had been in Colorado, so none of the churches knew him. However, I had been in the area for several years, so occasionally, when he met people, they would say, "You must be Terry's Dad."

He was always proud to affirm that truth. It was funny because whenever I went to Colorado, people would say to me, "You must be Bill Austin's son."

Now the shoe was on the other foot, but it didn't stay that way long. His passion for the church soon became noticeable; it didn't take long before people were once again saying, "You must be Bill Austin's son" whenever I came around.

He did that for as long as he was physically able. It got to where he was simply worn out. He had pushed himself as far as one leg would carry him. Toward the end, he told me several times that he was tired. I think that's what finally did him in at the end; he wore out. He gave everything he had to serve God and the church.

In the last 20 years of his work before retirement, he was an employee of the Baptist denomination and worked with numerous churches. His job was to provide resources, training, encouragement, and guidance. I don't know the precise numbers, but he worked with 50 or 60 churches spread out across half the state of Colorado. He knew every church intimately, visiting with them frequently. He not only knew the pastors; he knew the church people as well. He helped start many of the churches, and with others, he was key to survival when they were about to go under.

The last few years of his life were difficult because of what he saw happening in the church. He never quit attending and supporting and especially praying for the church. But he was saddened to see pastors build their own kingdom and music programs that were little more than concerts for singers with big egos. He grieved over Bible study being replaced by small groups that "shared ignorance," in his words. The church had changed, and it broke his heart.

Daddy taught me to love the church. He also taught me the importance of doing church the right way. In a sense, I'm glad that he's no longer around to see what has happened to the church. Daddy supported Billy Graham's ministry, although he was disappointed with how they worked with local churches during a Denver crusade. However, he would be appalled to see what Graham's son has done by using the ministry as a political tool.

It would also be difficult for Daddy to comprehend how preachers can stand in the pulpit and proclaim the name of a politician instead of Jesus. Although Daddy loved the church, he wasn't overly patient with preachers. He saw many abuse their role and influence to stroke their own ego. He understood that church was people, primarily the person in the pew struggling to get through life. He was into building up people, not constructing a large institution.

I must confess that although Daddy taught me how to love the church without promoting everything done in the name of the church, I'm not sure he would be pleased with where I have landed in my relationship with the church. I have always loved the church, and I still love the church. However, I've walked away from the institutional church. I got fed up with the lavish entertainment, celebrity preachers, outlandish facilities, and political pandering, so the obvious conclusion was this is not the church that elicited Christ's sacrifices.

Daddy would not have left the church with me, but he would have certainly spoken out about what is happening. I currently belong to a home church group of great folks. We gather to encourage one another in our Christian walk in fulfillment of Hebrews 10:24-25: "...and let us consider how to stimulate one another to love and good deeds, not forsaking our own assembling together, as is the habit of some, but encouraging *one another*; and all the more as you see the day drawing near."

The majority of my writing is about the church because I still care. It saddens me to watch Christians turn away from Jesus' teachings to support politicians who promise them financial rewards. It's extremely discouraging to see preachers chase after prestigious pulpits.

As we were striving to find a church where we could comfortably belong, Sharon and I visited numerous churches in our neighborhood. We were offered countless cups of coffee and donuts, but not once did anyone reach out to know us. We always came home with slick printed material but never with the name of anyone who cared. Even when we filled out the visitor forms, the only follow up we ever received was an occasional email written like a sales pitch from a local insurance firm.

The way Daddy taught me to love the church was to love the people. The reason he was not at home after dinner most evenings was because that's when he went to visit people. Current members, new members, visitors, or just people in the community. It's incomprehensible that anyone could visit the church without meeting him and without him following up to learn how he could be a friend.

The only way to love the church is to love people because the church is people. The church is not a building, an institution, a program, activity, or ministry—it is people. The church in America has forgotten this truth. At some point in time, I think it was probably in my lifetime, doing the work of the church changed from ministering to people to building large structures. It has arrived at the point where a sizable portion of people who attend church have no contact with anyone else. They sit in a theater seat next to strangers, listen to musicians as if they are at a concert, and watch a sermon on an oversized screen. They are then ushered out quickly so the next group can be herded in. That's not the church that Jesus bought with His sacrifice.

The reason Jesus gave Himself for the church is clearly spelled out, "...that He might present to Himself the church in all her glory, having no spot or wrinkle or any such thing; but that she would be holy and blameless" (Ephesians 5:27). He didn't give himself to have multi-million-dollar buildings, children's playlands, world-renowned preachers, or even electrifying musical performances. His goal was to have people who are "holy and blameless."

A sizable portion of the church that we are expected to love has no interest in what God wants. Instead, the church celebrates men who are greedy for power and money, elevates personalities who can mesmerize an audience, lavishes gifts on preachers of health and wealth without any regard for caring for the poor or loving one another. Daddy taught me how to love the people, not the institution.

During my childhood, most summers, we made the trip from Colorado to Texas to visit relatives. Both of my parents were raised near Amarillo, and Mama, especially, had numerous relatives living in the city. They also had some family friends in the area that we often visited as well.

One of those friends was B.L. Davis. Daddy and B.L. had been longtime friends, and both served in the military during the war. Daddy went to the Pacific and B.L. to Europe. Both came home wounded. As I've already described, Daddy's wounds required the loss of his right leg. B.L.'s injuries were psychological and not as noticeable.

In the summers, when we visited B.L., he was doing well and serving as the pastor of a healthy church. I had no idea he ever had any issues. What I remember from those visits is homemade ice cream and watermelon. Together, Daddy and B.L. could easily consume a sizable watermelon.

Many years later, when I was working for the Texas Baptist denomination, I frequently spoke at meetings and worked with numerous churches and pastors. I was speaking to a group of pastors and retired pastors in Waco, and during a lunch break, B.L. Davis sat next to me at the table. He and Daddy were still friends, although they didn't see each other often.

While we ate lunch, B.L. told me something I had never heard before. He said, "Terry, your Dad saved my life several times."

I had no idea what he was talking about, and obviously, Daddy had never said anything about such a thing. He went on to describe how messed up he was when he returned from the war. He had a drinking problem and spent a lot of nights in bars. He told me how Daddy frequently went looking for him and dragged him home. He said if Daddy had not continually come to his rescue, he would have surely died in one of those bars.

It was great to hear someone talk about my Dad like that, but to be honest, I did not have any difficulty believing it. Daddy frequently went out of his way to meet the needs of other people.

He loved church people enough to do whatever was necessary to help. He also loved them enough to correct them when they went astray. I remember one young man in one of Daddy's churches who felt like God wanted him to preach. C.J. was an unusual guy, not many friends, and many problems with his family. The most notable feature about C.J. was his lack of hygiene. He stunk, and sometimes he stunk bad. Daddy looked him in the eye and told him if we was going to work with people, he needed to take a shower every day and clean himself up. You don't say something like that to someone unless you really dislike them, or you love them and care.

Jesus sacrificed so B.L. could find victory over his wartime trauma and drinking problem. He sacrificed so C.J. would learn what was necessary to relate to people. He sacrificed so all of us can be holy and blameless. That is when we can feel good about the church.

The church has undergone significant transition during my lifetime. It has gone from being primarily a community organization to a regional mega-institution. It has gone from being controlled by consistent, long-term residents in a community to being controlled by paid professionals and recruited staff. It has gone from being held together by relationships to being held together by slick programming and religious fads.

That transition isn't complete. The current church model of mega-churches with enormous facilities, expensive programming, and ego-driven preaching is not sustainable. The first blow will be financial costs. However, the blow that might prove to be fatal is the loss of relationships. People sit for 60 minutes in a large crowd without getting to know one another. Remember, the purpose of gathering is to exhort and encourage one another. It's not possible when there are no longer any "one anothers."

Even though the church goes through transitions, it will not disappear. God loves the church so much that He sent His Son as a sacrifice. I'm not able to explain all the ramifications of what that means other than the fact that it's ample evidence He will do whatever is needed for the church to survive. Although I've given up on the institutional church, I still have great love for God's people. It saddens me to see them distracted by political agendas and greedy hucksters. Jesus warned about this happening when He said, "Beware of the false prophets, who come to you in sheep's clothing, but inwardly are ravenous wolves" (Matthew 5:17).

During the 2,000 year plus history of the church, similar things have happened with the church. Because of His love, God has preserved the church. I'm striving to follow Daddy's lead by loving the people of the church.

Conclusion

One of my earliest memories is being in the backyard of our house in the small town of Eads, Colorado. We moved to this farming community when I was two years old and stayed for four years. I have a lot of good memories of that place, but my earliest is not pleasant. My sister and I were playing in the yard. I was riding in a push car, and she was providing mobility. My father came home with two live chickens in a sack.

Daddy was the pastor of the Baptist Church in town. It was his first church, and he might have been their first pastor, I'm not sure. He had to drop out of college in Texas prior to finishing because of family obligations, primarily my polio. From the stories I've heard over the years, our family was barely surviving financially, but I don't ever remember feeling like we were poor. We never went hungry or without clean clothes.

The church didn't have the resources to pay the pastor a decent salary, so families would supplement with stuff other than money. On this occasion, it was chickens.

Daddy removed the birds from the burlap sack, and with a small hatchet, he whacked off their heads. Both he and Mama grew up on a farm, so I'm sure they didn't think anything about what was happening.

I remember two headless chickens flopping around all over the backyard. It was a memorable sight, and Linda and I were both frightened, so she quickly pushed me in my car around the house, back to the front yard. I can still see two feather-covered animal torsos hopping and flopping around uncontrollably with blood spurting into the air. It is one of my earliest memories, and it's certainly my first memory of being afraid.

It's somewhat ironic that the cause of my first fear was Daddy. I can't think of any other time that he caused me to be afraid, except for what happened 58 years later. He died a little more than eight years ago, and I wasn't ready.

Although he taught me a lot about God, I felt like there was still much to learn. What I've discovered in the past eight years is not that I needed to learn more; I needed to rely on what I already knew. It was time for me to apply the truths I already knew.

A few weeks ago, I had lunch with my good friend Charlie. He's a good friend because he will take time away from his busy schedule to pick me up and take me to lunch. We always have a great time. Charlie knows how I feel about my father. He drove several hours to attend Daddy's funeral because he knew how important it was to me.

After our long lunch, Charlie drove me back home. As we were getting out of the van, he told me that his wife asked him if my life was hard, and he wasn't sure how to answer. Charlie and I have always been honest with each other, so I told him the truth—my life is hard. It gets harder with each passing day. However, I quickly added that I have enjoyed nearly every day of my life. I would never characterize my life as unhappy. In fact, anyone who knows me will testify that I am a happy, content person. I seldom complain about circumstances or plead with God to change anything in my life.

I resonate with the words of Paul in one of my favorite passages: "Not that I speak from want, for I have learned to be content in whatever circumstances I am. I know how to get along with humble means, and I also know how to live in prosperity; in any and every circumstance I have learned the secret of being filled and going hungry, both of having abundance and suffering need. I can do all things through Him who strengthens me. Nevertheless, you have done well to share *with me* in my affliction" (Philippians 4:11-14).

When we examine Paul's life, it's clear that misery was a common experience. The second time he is mentioned in the scripture, he was struck blind and had to be led by the hand. After God restored his eyesight, he spent three years in the wilderness seminary, preparing for his life work. That work involved great danger and risk. Here's how he described his life: "...in far more labors, in far more imprisonments, beaten times without number, often in danger of death. Five times I received from the Jews thirty-nine *lashes*. Three times I was beaten with rods, once I was stoned, three times I was shipwrecked, a night and a day I have spent in the deep. *I have been* on frequent journeys, in dangers from rivers, dangers from robbers, dangers from *my* countrymen, dangers from the Gentiles, dangers in the city, dangers in the wilderness, dangers on the sea, dangers among false brethren; *I have been* in labor and hardship, through many sleepless nights, in hunger and thirst, often without food, in cold and exposure. Apart from *such* external things, there is the daily pressure on me *of* concern for all the churches" (2 Corinthians 11:23-28).

The experiences of Paul would fill a complete season of adventures on Netflix. Remember, this is the same man who said, "I have learned to be content in whatever circumstances I am." Many would have been broken and discouraged by similar experiences. We don't hear about them because they gave up. Paul claims to have learned the "secret" of having abundance as well as going hungry.

The Greek word translated "have learned the secret" speaks of being initiated or instructed in sacred mysteries. Within the context used by Paul, it speaks of being disciplined or taught via a practical lesson. The tense suggests a past process that taught him how to accept the experiences of life.

As I've tried to say throughout this book, I learned that same contentment. I had many teachers along the way and endured many experiences as well, but the primary instructor for me was my earthly father.

My earliest memory of Daddy was when he frightened me by whacking off the heads of two chickens. The only other time Daddy caused fear in my life was when my brother called to tell me that Daddy had died. Of course, my first reaction was intense grief. As Sharon hugged me, I sobbed like a child. It wasn't long however, before that sorrow turned to concern and then to fear.

It was fear that I wasn't ready to handle life, that I still had much more to learn. I wasn't sure I was ready. What would I do now that I had nobody to call with questions or needs? I confess, I still frequently catch myself wanting to pick up the phone and give him a call. I need to talk to him about something or share a joy, but he's not there.

However, during the past eight years, I have learned that I was ready. There have been numerous challenges and difficult situations, but Daddy taught me well. I do not doubt that

> God will never ask me to do anything I can't do.
> God made the ultimate sacrifice for me.
> God is worthy of reverence.
> God is consistent.
> God is love.
> Faith is the greatest gift from God.
> God loves the church.

When I became a parent, it was more and more evident that most of what I needed to know about God and my relationship to life came from my father. As my three sons grew up, I wanted to be able to do the same thing for them, so I began to think about Daddy's teaching method. How did he teach me all this stuff?

I can assure you that it wasn't through lectures. He was not the kind to lecture. Certainly, we talked over the years, but he taught me about the heavenly father by the way he lived. I didn't need a lecture on faith because daily, I could see how a man of faith lived. Giving an outline about trusting God was unnecessary because he showed me what it meant to trust God.

This approach fits the pattern of Scripture. Remember, in the 11th chapter of Hebrews where we are given a precise definition of faith. In order to make the meaning clear, the writer points us to example after example of people who lived by faith. If you want to know what faith is, then look at Cain, and Enoch, and Noah, and Abraham, and numerous others who are the characters in stories we have told over and over for centuries. The best way to understand God is to examine the lives who already know Him.

That is what my father did for me. He knew God, and when I watched him, I learned what God was all about.

Many years ago, I established the life goal of being half the man my father was. I fear that I've fallen short, but I'm still trying.

I've also tried to be the man who can teach my three sons what God is like. I want them to know God like their grandfather knew God.

Appendix: Bill Austin's Eulogy

And we know that all things work together for good to them that love God, to them who are the called according to his purpose. For whom he did foreknow, he also did predestinate to be conformed to the image of his Son, that he might be the firstborn among many brethren. Moreover whom he did predestinate, them he also called: and whom he called, them he also justified: and whom he justified, them he also glorified. What shall we then say to these things? If God be for us, who can be against us? He that spared not his own Son, but delivered him up for us all, how shall he not with him also freely give us all things? Romans 8:28-32 (KJV)

About a dozen years ago on the evening of the Fourth of July, I was sitting with my father at a picnic. The entire extended family was there at the Glorieta Conference Center near Santa Fe, New Mexico. Because of the holiday, the conference leaders choose to have a barbeque picnic with patriotic music and festivities, honoring our nation. I was especially proud when they had members of the various military branches stand up. When they called for the Marines to stand, I helped steady my father's portable lawn chair as he stood proud.

As he aged, it was more and more difficult for Daddy to stand up straight, but on this particular occasion he was as tall as I remembered when I was a kid. Daddy's size was something that always impressed me. I don't know if it was because I was so small and weak, but I considered him to be the strongest man around. As young children, I remember both Linda and I trying to arm wrestle him but we could never even move his strong right arm.

It is not surprising that when it comes to remembering and honoring his life, strength is the first thing that comes to mind. Not only did Daddy stand strong, but he was the source of strength for so many other people.

It is hard to comprehend the amount of courage he possessed as he and his fellow Marines stormed the beaches of Iwo Jima. On that seemingly inconsequential volcano in the middle of the Pacific Ocean, he suffered a loss that forever changed his life and impacted the lives of everyone who knew him. A mortar blast led to the eventual amputation of his right leg and one of the defining moments of his life.

More than three years in and out of the hospital, a tragic automobile accident in downtown Amarillo, a tornado ravaging their home just a few days after Linda's birth, the emotional struggle of dealing with the devastating effects of polio on his oldest son – none of these events deterred him, they only served to give him additional strength.

Daddy loved his family but he loved the church even more. I don't say that with regret or condemnation. Serving the church was his life. He heard God's call to the ministry in 1951 when he had a wife and two very young children, no education, no experience, and no money. He went off to college but he didn't have time to finish before God led him to pastor a little church in a nondescript town in southeastern Colorado.

He gathered that small congregation in an auto garage. He joked more than once that they were the only church in town with a grease rack. Daddy went to work repairing shoes, a task he knew nothing about, but it was an opportunity to supplement the meager income from preaching. He built that church into a strong congregation and as far as I know it still stands today, sixty years later.

He then took his family to the town of Monte Vista, located deep in the Rocky Mountains. At least this church had a meeting place but it was a one room building about the size of a good bedroom. We went to Sunday School in cars in the parking lot. If you were a visitor you might be told that your class met in the blue Buick on the north side of the building. He literally built a new building for this church, which was quite a feat given Daddy's carpentry skills. I remember one time he told me the only difference between a screw and a nail was that you can remove a screw.

Next stop was East Side Baptist Church in Colorado Springs. It was called East Side because the building was on the last street on the east side of town. The parsonage was next door to the church and we often had Sunday School classes meeting in our basement. I will always remember this church because this is where Daddy baptized me one Sunday evening. I can remember someone picking me up and handing me to Daddy standing in the water. He held me in his arms, placed me on a stool in the water, and baptized me. It was one of the proudest moments of my life.

Years later when this church was celebrating an anniversary or a milestone of some sort, they invited Daddy and other former pastors to the celebration. They told him that after reading through the church minutes it was discovered there were several Sundays when Daddy didn't get paid – the church did not have the money. They made up for it that day and gave Daddy a nice check. He was grateful for the gesture and the money, although he did say he needed the money a lot more back then than he did now.

From Colorado Springs, Daddy took his family to Thornton, a suburb of Denver. First Baptist Church was the largest church Daddy served and at the time, one of the largest Baptist churches in the entire state. Steve was born while we lived there and I remember having to share a bedroom with a little brother, although he was not my "little" brother for long. During this pastorate Daddy became very active with Colorado Baptists and was placed in several positions of responsibility and honor. It was not surprising that others recognized his great strength.

This was Daddy's last full-time church to pastor, moving next to serve dozens of churches in Eastern Colorado as an Area Missionary. He was extremely well-known, liked, and respected. It was always an honor for me when I would meet someone in one of Daddy's churches and they would quickly identify me as "Bill Austin's son." Years later, after I had been a pastor in the Texas panhandle, Daddy and Mama moved to Amarillo. Whenever Daddy would visit a church they would say to him, "You must be Terry Austin's father." However, that did not last long. Soon it was reversed and people were again saying to me, "You must be Bill Austin's son." I have never been embarrassed by that designation.

Perhaps the greatest asset that I have to help me be successful was Daddy. Because he managed with one leg, he understood what it took to accomplish things with a decided disadvantage. I remember asking him one time if he wished he had his leg. He said no, with no reservation in his voice. His answer confused me for many years and I eventually learned that he knew it was a defining experience of his life.

He never allowed me to make excuses or take a shortcut. When Mama wanted me to go slow and not take a risk, Daddy pushed me out the door. I remember him saying more than once, "If you fall down we'll pick you up!" And he did, every time.

The only time I ever remember Daddy getting angry was when a Cub Scout leader came to our home in Colorado Springs and told us I could not join the Scouts; they were not equipped to deal with a kid in a wheelchair.

Daddy literally taught me how to trust. Because I could not walk up and down stairs and it was difficult for Daddy to carry me up and down stairs, he would get at the bottom of the steps and tell me just to fall and he would catch me. That might be easy for a six year old, but trust me; it's not easy when you are fourteen or fifteen.

At the age of twenty-one, I mustered up the courage one Sunday evening to tell Daddy that I felt like God was calling me to be a preacher. Once I told him I was confident there would be no backing out. I knew he would encourage me, but I was surprised when he said, "I've known it for a long time."

As I neared graduation from seminary, Daddy called one day and asked if I was interested in pastoring a church in Colorado. That had been my plan all along and I knew that if Daddy just said, "My son is ready to be a pastor," a church would call me. He said I would need to complete a questionnaire that he asked of all his prospective pastors. When I returned the completed form, he sent it back to me along with a letter explaining that I had answered a couple of the questions incorrectly. We had some theological differences that neither one of us was willing to overlook so I never served a church in Colorado.

This really illustrates one of Daddy's greatest qualities – he never wavered from his convictions, even when it was inconvenient. It might seem that he was being unreasonable or mean-spirited. But the reality is that he was willing to act on his beliefs. I was disappointed about not getting to pastor in Colorado, but I am proud that he was unwilling to violate his convictions for my convenience.

But our differences were never a problem between us. Daddy never made you feel unworthy if you disagreed with him. When I finally did become a pastor (in Texas, not Colorado), Daddy was always the first and only person I called when I had a problem or a question. After awhile, I realized his advice was always the same, regardless of the problem or situation. All he ever told me was to "love the people." I could never do it as good as he did but it was always the correct advice.

Loving church people might have been what Daddy did best. I remember as a kid how he always embarrassed us when we went to a restaurant or somewhere a group of people were gathered. He could walk into a room not knowing anyone but walk out having spoken to everyone. He told me once that is was difficult for him because he was basically a shy person. Few people would ever know that he was shy.

I know people felt loved by him because for years he has constantly had people contact him to see how he is doing. Folks he had not heard from in years. People who were in one of his churches. He was always telling about someone who called or came by. People felt drawn to "Brother Bill."

In spite of the fact I was not doctrinally sound enough to pastor one of his churches, Daddy always supported my ministry. He came and preached a revival for us in the Texas panhandle. He knew that I had been trying unsuccessfully for years to get one hundred people together for a Sunday service. About midway through the revival, he began telling the folks that we should try to have a hundred people in church on Sunday morning. That's all he did - no big promotion or slogan, just a simple reminder. Sure enough, on Sunday morning we had a hundred people there. The first and only time in my thirteen year ministry at that church.

Daddy was always proud of all his kids. When you spoke with him on the phone he was quick to let you know what was going on with the others. He always knew what was happening with Linda in Colorado, he kept in touch with Steve's baseball exploits (in fact, in the final week he called Steve to see how an Arizona tournament was going), and he knew Jeff's family schedule and kept up with all their activities.

Whenever I write a book, Daddy buys them by the box and gives them away to friends and people he meets. He always loved to call and tell me that someone told him they read one of my books and they said it was the best book they ever read. It seemed to give Daddy more pride than me.

That is what I will miss most about Daddy. Those once a week phone calls asking how I'm doing and what's new in our lives. It will be hard when my next problem arises and I will not be able to call Daddy and ask him what to do. Nor will I hear him say, "It will be ok, God will take care of it."

I think that is why Daddy was so strong - his unwavering faith in God! He had learned, through some very hard lessons, that God will take care of everything. He taught me how to trust God, the most valuable lesson a father can give to a son. The reason I was able to understand this truth is that I knew if God ever did fail, Daddy would be there to pick me up and help me start over.

When a loved one dies, the family usually selects a memento to remind them of the person they lost. That will not be necessary for me. When I was seventeen years old, the doctor put me through a long ordeal in order to do a spinal fusion to help ease the complications caused by polio. The plan was to chisel some bone from my thigh and lay it next to my spine so it would grow into a solid piece. At the last moment, the doctor decided I did not have enough bone for the surgery. Without hesitation, Daddy offered bone from his only leg and it is been a part of my backbone for forty-four years. It is the only reminder I need of his sacrificial love.

At that Fourth of July rally in New Mexico, Daddy turned to me and asked if I would preach his funeral when he died. I immediately said, "Let's don't talk about that, you're not going to die."

However, as I thought about it, I realized what he was saying. Before we left the picnic I told him I would be honored to preach his funeral. In fact, I can't think of anyone who would do a better job.

The main goal in my life has always been the same – to be half the man Daddy was.

In our final conversation, just a few days before he died, I asked Daddy if he was concerned about the outcome of a biopsy. Without any reservation in his voice,

Daddy said he was not worried. Then he added, "Romans 8:28 has always been true."

> *And we know that all things work together for good to them that love God, to them who are the called according to his purpose.*

The Author

Bill Austin was born in 1925. His oldest son was born, in the same month, 25 years later. Bill was pastor of four churches in Colorado, becoming more and more involved in denominational leadership as his career progressed. After 18 years of work as a local church pastor, he went to work for the Home Mission Board of the Southern Baptist Convention. He was an Area Missionary, working with more than 50 churches scattered across eastern Colorado. Upon retirement, he served as Interim Pastor for dozens of churches in the Texas panhandle.

His son Terry was also a pastor. He served a small Baptist church in the Texas panhandle for 13 years and later with a new church start in Fort Worth. Terry also worked for the Baptist General Convention of Texas and continued working as a church consultant for a total of 15 years. Currently, Terry is a full-time writer/ghostwriter and book publisher. This is his 26th written book and 100th book published through his publishing company.

In many ways, Bill and Terry had a typical father/son relationship. However, you will discover from this book that their relationship was unique in other ways. Perhaps the most significant commonality between them was their faith. *My Two Fathers* is about the origin of faith that was passed from father to son.

www.ingramcontent.com/pod-product-compliance
Lightning Source LLC
Chambersburg PA
CBHW072009090426
42734CB00033B/2138